Transforming Technology into Profit

A guide to leading new ideas through the complexities of the corporate world and transforming them into successful new products

Dr Andy Wynn

ISBN: 978-1-7927-3685-8

Copyright © 2018 Andy Wynn

All rights reserved. No part of this publication may be reproduced, stored in a retrieval system, or transmitted, in any form, or by any means (electronic, mechanical, photocopying, recording or otherwise) without the prior written permission of the publisher.

This book is sold subject to the condition that it shall not, by way of trade or otherwise, be lent, hired out, or otherwise circulated without the publisher's prior consent in any form of binding or cover other than that in which it is published and without a similar condition including this condition being imposed on the subsequent purchaser.

To read more about the information discussed in this book visit the Author's website; www.ttipconsulting.co.uk.

*This book is dedicated to my wife, Julie,
who has been the real secret to all my success over the years.*

CONTENTS

	Introduction	1
1	The Process of Transforming Technology into Profit	8
2	Barriers to Transforming Technology into Profit	34
3	Is it a good idea? – the art of idea selection	60
4	How to make your ideas real – the art of project management	102
5	How to take people with you – the art of leading and managing teams	134
6	Juggling all the balls – the art of portfolio management	155
7	On the home straight – the art of launching new products successfully	194
	Conclusion	218
	Acknowledgements	223
	About the Author	225

INTRODUCTION

This is a book about how to successfully lead new ideas through the maze of organisational structure and through the barriers of internal politics and turn them into sustainable profits for your business. During my 30 years in industry, I have read plenty of great books on innovation and new product development processes. I have sat through many good seminars and presentations explaining the mechanics of these processes. All very well thought out, well researched and presented. But whenever I went back to my day job and tried to implement what I had learnt, it was not easy. I discovered many barriers which slowed project progress, many challenges that prevented successful project implementation, and many negative attitudes that blocked or brought down great ideas. So I was motivated to write this book to fill in the gaps and bring a sense of realism to this important subject and to help all those thousands of businesses worldwide who are struggling with implementing these processes.

This book is particularly targeted at those leading new product and new business development in medium to large manufacturing enterprises, nationally or globally, which accounts for the vast majority of those out in industry working on new technologies. Though not specifically designed with individual entrepreneurs or small businesses in mind, as the same barriers may not apply, many of the principles in this book will still be useful. More broadly, it is also aimed at anyone working in a technologically based industrial company, particularly those involved in new business development, new product development, innovation and business leadership. I believe that if we can educate business and technology leaders not only in the process of innovation, but also in how to actually implement these processes in the real world, then the development of new products and technologies will become leaner, faster and we can begin to accelerate the delivery of new products and new functionalities, in turn growing profits, developing economies and improving the quality of life for all.

It is written by someone who has lived it first hand, someone who has built their whole career around 'Transforming Technology into Profit,' from both sides of the Technology fence, someone who has made enough mistakes and had enough successes along the way to understand what works and what does not. I make reference in this book to numerous examples of situations I met over the years with respect to the process of Transforming Technology into Profit (TTIP), each a challenge that had to be overcome. These are all real examples, with real people (though with no names to respect anonymity, confidentiality, and in some cases dignity). Some of these challenges I could deal with, some I am still learning how to deal with, some I was too young and naïve in my career to know how to deal with at the time. I do not try to hold myself up as perfect in this respect. The examples of behaviours in these situations, some displayed by myself, some displayed by others, serve only to illustrate that such situations are real, and that you will likely need to deal with them at some point in your career. How you deal with them will make a huge impact on how successful your business becomes at TTIP and on your own career, particularly as several of the barriers are not unique, and impact many other aspects of business.

Let me set the scene by defining what I mean by Technology. Technology is the practical application of science, so when I talk about technology in this book, I am referring broadly to all existing and new innovations that have an underlying basis in science to make them work. So for me, technology means new engineering designs, new materials, new devices, new systems, and new software, all creating new functionality that didn't exist before. In the context of business, this encompasses a variety of business functions, including not only the classic R&D department, but also process engineering, application engineering, and several others that use technology as the base to deliver their work. So new technology can be a new furnace design, or a new semiconductor memory chip, a new aircraft design, or a new material, all of which deliver new functionality. This definition essentially applies to all industry, including petrochemical, automotive, aerospace, medical devices, metals, semiconductor, chemicals, agrochemicals, biotechnology, etc., and so this book should be relevant to you whichever industry you are working in, though generally the narrative is written from the perspective of Business-to-Business (B2B) markets, rather than Business-to Consumer (B2C) markets.

So why can a book on TTIP be relevant to any industry? Because this book is not a comprehensive guide on the New Product Development (NPD) process, rather this is a guide to how to make the NPD process work in the real world, in a real business, with real people. The classic NPD process is however woven throughout, forming the structure and framework for this book, and can be clearly followed throughout the narrative and the chapters.

Innovation is a much hyped word these days, and is certainly one of the latest business buzzwords. Everywhere you turn there are endless books published on the subject and there are many academic groups that study the processes in depth and come up with some very clever models of how to identify new ideas and business opportunities. There are also many great books published on the Product Development process, and I've read plenty in my time and worked with plenty of consultants and experts in the field, but my experience is that these generally focus exclusively on the mechanics of the process (which you certainly need), or, though insightful and thought provoking, are sometimes too complex, too academic, too clever and offer too many tools and techniques to really be useful in real world business situations by real people.

We are all working in increasingly complex market environments. In the business world we now talk about the VUCA environment (Volatile Uncertain Complex Ambiguous). Many of the more complex innovation and product development tools require data that are difficult or sometimes not possible to get, which only serves to devalue the output (Garbage In Garbage Out) and so the value of using them.

Whatever tools you choose to work with, above all you need to practice them. If I read a book on how to drive, does that mean I can drive a car? If I read a manual on how to fly a Boeing 747, does that mean I can get into the cockpit of a plane and fly passengers around? Of course not, it requires a lot of practice before you can successfully and safely put your knowledge into practice in the real world. NPD is no different, you can learn the mechanics of the processes and the multiple steps required, but you also need to learn the real world commercial and interpersonal skills that allow you to put it into practice successfully. Yes, the consequences of getting it wrong are not so dramatic and so devastating as if you get it wrong flying an aircraft, but they are no less important. Remember that your business is a bunch of people, they (and you) are there to earn money to put bread on the table and improve the quality of life for themselves and their families. How your business performs does not just affect you, it affects your dependants, and your communities. So for you to improve the quality of your life, you need your employment to be successful and for your employment to be successful you need your business to be successful. It never ceases to amaze me how much internal politics and infighting there are within businesses. It's a constant battle with human nature, and it takes maturity to realise that we are all in this together and will succeed or fail together, and we would all be wise to change our behaviour accordingly. If you are new to the world of work, you will learn very quickly that working within a business is all about the 3Ps; 'People, Politics and Process.'

This book attempts to look at Innovation and New Product Development processes in the broader context of how they fit into the wider business landscape. Without this appreciation, any Product Development Process will always struggle. So this book is primarily about how to work with people. It summarises what I have learnt over 30 years about how to take your expertise in your technological field and your expertise in project management and in innovation and the new product development process, and apply them in the real world of business. You might already be a renowned technical expert in your field or understand well the process of innovation, but if you don't know how to work within your own internal politics, you will struggle to deliver in your organisation.

I have had a long relationship with technology. Much of my career has been focused on developing new products, either directly or through management of new product and new business development programs and teams across the world. But I have also seen the world from the other side of the Technology fence at various times in my career, in general management roles, in operations, quality, sales and marketing roles and responsibilities. During my career, I have built factories, I have set up new businesses, and I have transferred production processes across continents. But in each of these roles I needed technology, whether as a provider or as a user. So I have lived first hand with the frustrations and challenges associated with delivering technology and dragging it through the complex organisational and operational networks of many businesses.

In some of the businesses I have worked with, innovation was left purely to the Technology department. There was a belief that new products come out of the R&D department and that the rest of the organisation just has to sit back and wait for new products to pop out occasionally. Happily, nowadays, most companies are enlightened enough to understand that innovation has to be a company-wide process to be successful, and that technologists play their part just as much as the sales team, operations team, and all the other business functions that need to come together to Transform Technology into Profit.

So this book is not a book just for technologists, it is for all business leadership. To successfully Transform Technology into Profit, all business leadership needs to be on board and understand how it all works. You cannot leave new product development to technologists, they contribute only part of the skills and process required. Understanding the process of innovation and how to manage new product development is just the first step, the real secret to success with TTIP is learning how to bring everyone else in the organisation with you.

I hope you find it useful.

Andy

CHAPTER 1

THE PROCESS OF TRANSFORMING TECHNOLOGY INTO PROFIT

Transforming Technology into Profit (TTIP) is a long and complex process. But like any complex process, much thought has gone into developing simple models of the process, with the intent of helping us put structure and order into the chaos and thus allow us to build systems and tools to try to manage the process in a more methodical way. At the core of TTIP is innovation and new product development, both of which have been studied and analysed for many decades, and so we have some robust and well known models to build our guide to TTIP on. One classic model for innovation is the innovation funnel, which has served as the basis for many industrial new product development systems, and which is taught at probably every course on innovation and new product development processes;

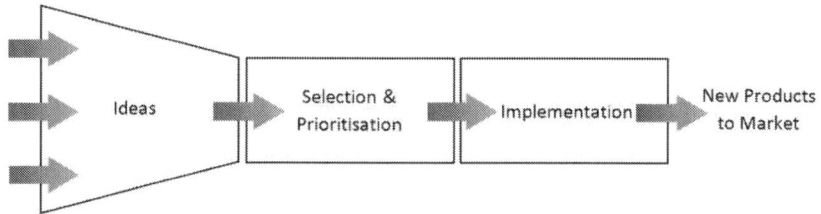

The Innovation Funnel and Variations

There are hundreds of different versions of the classic innovation funnel model, each with their own particular take on the approach and using different terminology for the parts of the funnel (just search for 'innovation funnel' on the internet and you will see what I mean), but at its most basic, the funnel consists of three sections. Section 1 is the funnel itself, where new ideas enter into the innovation process. As the funnel narrows, the ideas enter Section 2, where there is some mechanism for filtering all the ideas, and those which are selected as good ideas pass through to Section 3, where the ideas are implemented and become new products. This is a highly idealised model but forms a really useful basis to hang real world systems and processes off. There is absolutely nothing wrong with the innovation funnel, it's a great model, but as you will discover, it is only part of the picture, only part of the toolkit you will need to Transform Technology into Profit. I have worked with many colleagues over the years in several different businesses, on creating and refining TTIP processes, and the innovation funnel has usually featured somewhere in our thinking and our approach. Later in this book you will meet several tools and systems to help guide you through all the stages of TTIP, and this is how they hang together with respect to the innovation funnel;

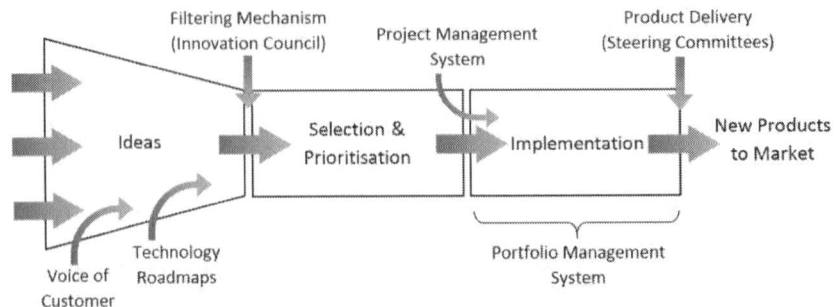

Using this model, you can start to see how complex the TTIP process really is, and why we have, and need, so many different processes and tools, but also, how they all fit together in sequence. As the process is long, it is vital to maintain relevance of your new product development project to your customers' needs throughout, and maintaining robust management and review processes all along the pipeline is the way to achieve that.

One of the processes that is core to managing the process of TTIP, is the Phase Gate review process, which is a fundamental project management technique that adds a set of go/no-go decision points into a project. We will explore the Phase Gate process in more detail in Chapter 4. Whilst it is not pure project management on its own (you will still need to use project planning tools in between the Phase Gates), the Phase Gate review approach is essential in overlaying clarity on whether a project really has progressed and how far. The innovation funnel and Phase Gate approaches have morphed together in many of the more recent versions of the innovation funnel.

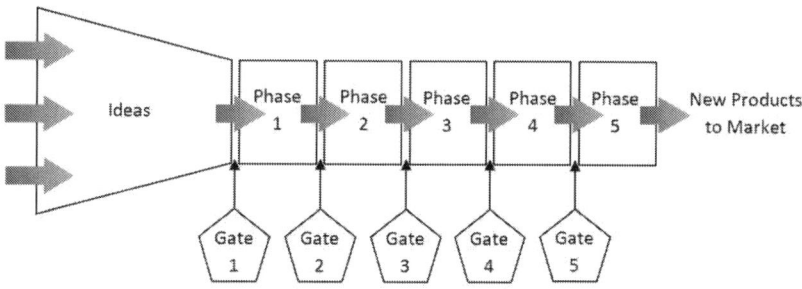

This version of the innovation funnel model gets a little closer to reality and allows better integration with the systems and tools we use to manage the process. It also introduces the concept that the Phase Gates are the filtering mechanism for the ideas and for project kill or proceed decisions along the pipeline. In reality, the funnel is not going to be a nice continuous smooth process as many of the published models suggest, as killing projects at the decision points will reduce the size of the pipeline in discrete jumps at each gate, so the real process is a series of filtering funnels, with as many downsizings of the pipeline as there are go/no go decision points in your innovation process. This modified version of the model shows more clearly why the percentage of ideas that make it to successful implementation is traditionally quite low (see later), as there are many review and decision points that an idea or project has to make it through before it can get to the end and into implementation.

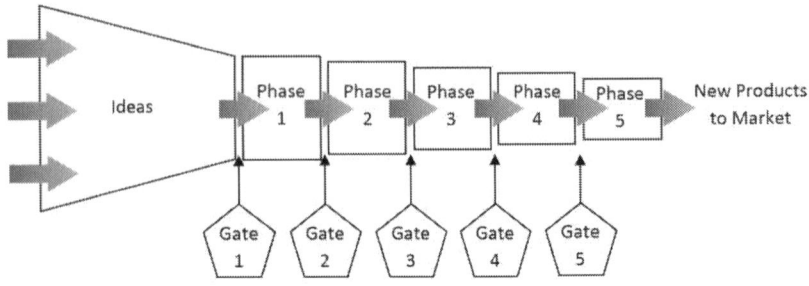

Another concept that I have found useful in visualising the modified filtering funnel model is that there are two axes to manage on this process. Along the x-axis, ideas turn into projects and these projects need close project management, but travelling down the pipeline at any one time will likely be many different projects (depending on the size and complexity of your business, the range of markets you address, and your business strategy), so along the y-axis, you will need to be managing a portfolio of projects, which requires different tools, a different skill set and a different approach. We will cover these two different aspects of project versus portfolio management in Chapters 4 & 6.

One immediate question that always gets asked when the innovation model is taught is 'how many ideas do you have to put into the funnel to get one successful project out?' I have heard various figures for this. One is a general rule of thumb that for every 7 ideas going into the funnel, 1 is likely to make it to successful implementation. This relates to the balance of ideas to projects in the pipeline that you need to maintain a healthy innovation pipeline (see later), but for me this only really relates to ideas/projects that are 'inside' the funnel. If you also consider ideas coming in and new products that have gone out to market (i.e. ideas and products outside the funnel), then the real ratio is going to be higher, much higher. For example, I heard one senior defence figure in the UK at a meeting in 2018 quote that 'of 1200 Defence projects funded by the UK government, only 8 had actually made it to implementation'. And this is just projects funded, which means they are already past the funnel stage, so the number of ideas that were generated to produce 1200 funded projects must have been many thousands. In a 1997 article '3,000 raw ideas = 1 commercial success!' published in the Research Technology Magazine [Stevens, G A. & Burley, J. 3,000 Raw Ideas Equals 1 Commercial Success!, Research Technology Management. 1997, 40-3, 1601-1703], the authors studied project and patent literature, plus venture capitalist experience, and they concluded that 'across most industries, it appears to require 3,000 raw ideas to produce one substantially new, commercially successful industrial product.' Like with most complex scenarios in business, there is undoubtedly no right answer. The actual ratio of ideas in, to new products out, will depend on how well your business is aligned with its innovation process, how deeply top management are involved, how resources are distributed down the innovation pipeline and maintaining the right balance of ideas/projects amongst the various steps of the process.

But what is the right balance? It is important to appreciate that the process of TTIP has to be a continuous process, with ideas constantly coming into the front end of the funnel and moving down the pipeline towards eventual implementation (if they ever reach that far). So it is important that you keep ideas flowing in and projects progressing, otherwise your pipeline will run dry and innovation will stop in your business. All of this requires process, process to keep ideas flowing into the funnel and processes at each point along the pipeline to manage ideas and projects. With respect to the three main sections of the funnel model (Ideas, Selection & Prioritisation, and Implementation), literature typically recommends maintaining around a 70%:20%:10% split, which reflects well the typical ratios I have worked with in businesses over the years.

We also need to consider that projects do sometimes make it to implementation, but never really fulfil their sales potential. We usually talk about such projects as being a 'technical success'. The reasons for this can be numerous; misdirected project targets at the start, not checking the targets against customer needs during project execution to see if anything had changed, lack of sales leadership and commitment to the new product, etc. I am sure we can all think of examples in our own businesses of such projects that were 'successfully' implemented but didn't deliver much profit.

Another approach to modifying the classic innovation funnel to make it fit into the real world has been to stand back and consider the environment within which the innovation funnel, and new product development processes, have to play out. In one approach, a group at the Cranfield School of Management have developed what they call the Pentathlon Framework, and have set their funnel inside the business environment of Strategy (in this case Innovation Strategy) and Culture (People and Organisation) [Innovation Management: Strategy and Implementation using the Pentathlon Framework Paperback, 2005, by Keith Goffin and Rick Mitchell].

However, as I said in my introduction, models and systems can get too complex for the real world. Experience has taught me that it is best to keep things simple. When you are working across departments and across functions, you soon discover that people have their own priorities, their own points of view and their own experiences. When you are working in a multi-national business, you will be working with different business cultures, where priorities and attitudes are different from your own, and with people whose first language is not English. The more complex the situation you find yourself working within, the more simple your approach needs to be in order to get a team contributing, to bring a team with you, and to make progress. And so I normally use my modified innovation filtering funnel model as a starting point to explain the process we will go through, the context within which it plays, and the tools we will use when starting a project. This is enough, because it is not an academic exercise in refining the innovation funnel or Phase Gate processes, we have a job to do, to Transform Technology into Profit.

But where should you start gathering ideas to go into the funnel? You need to start with your business strategy. If you are going to make a success of TTIP, then your business sure needs to have a strategy. Your business's strategy needs to be a set of clearly expressed guidelines about the direction and goals of the business, against which you can hold up any aspect of your business's work (not just new technology and new products) and make a decision on whether it fits the strategy or not and on how much it will contribute to achieving the goals. Importantly, it also needs to state what your business is not going to do, not just what it is going to do. Usually, it will define what markets you will work in and what markets you will avoid. It will state financial goals, including revenue and growth targets, and sometimes profit and other financial criteria, depending on what markets your business plays in and what your business is aiming to achieve. Business growth does not only come from new products of course, so your strategy should also give some indication about how the growth will be achieved in terms of the split between sales growth from new product sales versus organic market growth from existing products versus inorganic growth through acquisitions.

Organisational structure and the importance of functional interfaces

Another important aspect people need to appreciate if they are to be successful in TTIP is how their role fits in with the wider organisation, i.e. which cog they are, in the machine of the business. When you appreciate what your role is there to do, and what it is not there to do, you can more effectively play your part. Yes, people understand there are R&D departments, there are sales departments, there is operations and finance, etc., but people rarely appreciate how all these interconnect, where ownership lies and where they need to support each other, and most importantly, where shared ownership is required, because that's where the magic happens. Job descriptions are a good starting point for this, but we all know that the boundaries of job descriptions and role responsibilities can get quite fuzzy. In smaller organisations, it is normal that people take on a wider set of responsibilities (hence the phrase 'to wear many hats') than in larger organisations. This is great for personal growth and learning but can make it more challenging to know where one person's job ends and another begins. This can lead to the classic problem of things 'falling between the cracks' if no one takes responsibility for an action because they thought it was some else's job.

A culture of taking on several roles at once can be a good opportunity for a young ambitious person to take on more of the action, but can lead to conflict if they start overlapping activities with someone else in the organisation. A similar challenge occurs when moving between businesses and between business cultures in your career. I found exactly this when I moved from a smaller ($60m turnover) business (where I had multiple responsibilities) to a larger ($350m turnover) business part way through my career. I was used to having multiple responsibilities, and taking on more, as a way to further my career. I took this attitude into my new role in the bigger company and almost from day one I found myself treading on people's toes around the organisation. After several weeks of observing some quite negative reactions, I discovered how unpopular this was making me with some of my new colleagues and so I quickly changed my approach to focussing more on the boundaries inherent within my job description. By not appreciating my part in the new organisation, I was creating negative attitudes, and affecting progress on several fronts. This is how I learnt that you need to understand your place in the business if you want the process of TTIP to run as effectively as possible.

Transforming science and technology into products and delivering them to customers requires effective management of the functional interfaces within our business to clarify ownership of each stage of the process and facilitate collaboration. And so, not only does a person need to understand their position in their department and in their wider organisation, they also need to understand the part their departmental function plays within the business, and most importantly for TTIP, how their business function interfaces with others. To help people appreciate this, I have developed a simple model over the years of an industrial manufacturing business and how business functions interact and overlap with each other, as shown below.

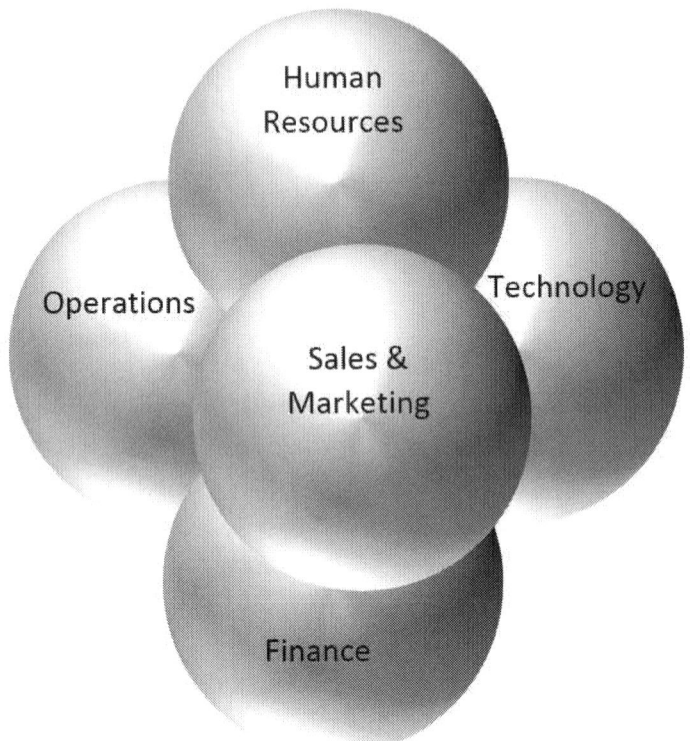

Many businesses build great competences in their underlying business functions, yet still fail to get their business to work effectively. This is because not only do we need good functional skills, we also need those functions to work effectively together for the whole business to work.

In the context of New Product Development, for simplicity, let's just look at the three middle functions in the model; Operations, Technology and Sales & Marketing. These three are all critical business functions, but TTIP success will only come if they work effectively and efficiently together in those areas where their responsibilities overlap (see below).

This is essentially about managing 'collaboration' (another business buzz word these days), and these interfaces between the functions are critical to making collaboration effective. The first step to getting the three functions to work together effectively is for those with functional responsibilities to understand and accept that these functional interfaces represent areas of shared responsibilities and that different functions need to take leadership on different aspects of the processes involved.

Application Engineering – the Technology / Sales & Marketing Interface;

If we focus first on the interface between the Technology and Sales & Marketing functions, this is what is known as

'Application Engineering'. Application Engineering as a function (rather than as a role, see later), encompasses all the activities that Technology and Sales & Marketing teams naturally work together on. Some of these activities tend to be technology driven exercises (e.g. non-standard product bespoking, reformulations of existing products, new designs) and some tend to be sales driven (e.g. product selection for customer applications, designs with existing products), and to help effective management of this interface function (and not let things fall between the cracks), it is important that the right person takes the lead, and the ownership, in these activities. Such roles can be assigned in projects by the project manager or by functional heads.

I will expand more on this function in Chapter 3, but I have seen first-hand what a critical role an Application Engineer plays in interpreting customer needs and acting as an effective liaison between Technology, Sales departments and customers. In the past, Technology and Sales teams would attempt to handle this function between them (or let it fall between the cracks in some cases), but in recent years the role of Application Engineer has become a standalone role in its own right and I believe this represents a pivotal change in our organisations, in orienting them towards more successful new product development and commercialisation.

Process Engineering – the Technology / Operations Interface;

The second interface area that has a big influence on TTIP is the interface between the Technology and Operations functions, this is 'Process Engineering.' It depends how your organisation is structured, but process engineering as a function tends to come under Manufacturing or wider operations line management, but is an area that requires special focus because I have seen on occasion how the process engineering function can head off in their own direction, in their quest for improving process efficiencies, sometimes in conflict with technology and R&D priorities.

The function of Process Engineering, encompasses all the activities that technology and operations teams naturally work together on, such as new process developments to create new products, improvements in product quality, cost reduction initiatives through product reformulation or raw material changes etc., and process efficiency improvements. Things do not tend to fall between the cracks in this interface because the operations team tends to lead historically on all these types of activities, but the danger I have observed is when operations start leading projects on new process development (because they have the engineering skills), when the project is intended to deliver a fundamentally new product or new functionality or delivers a fundamental change to an existing product. This is dangerous because the project becomes process lead (i.e. internally focused), instead of customer lead (i.e. externally focused), and project meetings can get almost entirely taken over by discussions on the nuts and bolts of the engineering designs, with the effect it is going to have on the product and functionality almost taking a back seat. I have witnessed such projects spiralling down into pissing contests, with team factions emerging around 'my design is better than your design.' Everything always comes back to people and politics.

Once again, as with the other functional interfaces, if you want a successful outcome on these shared activities, you need to appreciate what is happening in the dynamics of your organisation, look outward to put your customers first, and assign the correct functional leadership to such projects such that they do not get side-tracked by internal views of the world. Projects focused on delivering operational and quality improvements should remain operationally lead, but projects that utilise new process developments to deliver new product developments should be led by someone who can keep the product functionality, the customer and the end user right at the top of their agenda.

Product Management – the Operations / Sales & Marketing Interface;

To complete the picture, let's look at the interface between the Operations and Sales & Marketing functions, which is Product Management. I have seen the role of Product Manager used in a variety of ways in different businesses, with the role being pitched at differing levels of seniority. Organisationally, the role is generally under the Sales or Marketing function and can be reporting into Sales management or vice versa. In some organisations, I have seen the Product Manager effectively be the business unit manager for the product range they are responsible for, with end of line responsibility for pricing, and at the other extreme I have seen them used as technical support roles for sales people, with no pricing responsibility at all. The Product Management function tends to be focused on managing existing products and their day to day delivery to customers, almost like a supply chain role. Ideally, the Product Manager should have a broad understanding of the industry and markets they are serving, and is normally the best person to represent the customer in your new product development portfolio. They are also normally the best person to take ownership of Technology Roadmap exercises in their market segment (see Chapter 3).

I hope given the simple functional interface model you have seen and the examples I have raised on how things can go wrong, that you can now appreciate that understanding and management of the functional overlap areas are absolutely crucial in delivering effective collaboration between departments and between teams when working together to deliver projects. Having an appreciation of the range of activities that are shared and knowing when to take ownership or hand it over are high level management skills that will stand you in good stead in your career.

You may have noticed that there is another functional interface region in the simple model above that we have not yet mentioned. This is the area right in the centre, where all of the three key business functions of Technology, Operations and Sales & Marketing overlap, but not only that, all the three interface regions we have already discussed overlap here as well. This is the sweet spot, this is where the magic happens. If you can get all of these functions working truly in harmony, all pulling together in the same direction, then you will be delivering growth. This central region is New Business Development, so I like to call this region 'Transforming Technology into Profit'.

The functional business model described above, can be applied to any scale of industrial, technologically based manufacturing business, whether it is a small single site company, a multi-site national company, or a large multi-national with multiple divisions. The basic structure of this functional model will always be present in any of these scales and complexity of business, but the split of resources present between each of the functions and functional interfaces will vary as different business decisions are made by senior management in relation to driving the organisation towards delivering the business strategy, or a change in business strategy.

As any business grows in scale and multi-site complexity, there is however a further dimension to organisational structure that overlays the functional model, and which is also very important to appreciate if you want to be successful in TTIP. With additional complexity, at some point of critical mass, inevitably there comes a corporate centre (or headquarters), which has to be there to deal with the corporate governance requirements of the group legal entity, and although in modern businesses this tends to be physically relatively small compared to in the past, it does inevitably bring along with it a 'matrix' organisation. When your business is of the scale that it needs a corporate headquarters, and for multi-nationals, regional headquarters as well, then a whole extra layer (or two in the case of regional headquarters) of senior management appears. Understanding where your role fits in the matrix organisation is important in terms of knowing how to handle the People, Politics and Processes.

In such cases, every person in your organisation has to deal with demands coming from global versus regional versus local levels of the matrix, whether directly or indirectly, and in plenty of organisations, some of these demands appear to be in conflict rather than complimentary. It is the goal of any mature and sophisticated business to have a robust business strategy that it cascades down effectively to all employees, to attempt to get everyone pulling in the same direction. But in reality, this communication is not always perfect and messages can become distorted. Individuals can (sometime unintentionally) distort the message, or have their own agenda, which leads to conflicting demands on individuals within the matrix organisation.

If you consider the functional model described earlier, within the context of a matrix organisation, you will typically have a site functional manager (reporting to the site general manager), a regional functional manager (reporting to a regional Managing Director) and a global functional director (reporting to the CEO). All of these individuals need to understand clearly what their functions are, communicate regularly, respect reporting lines, and avoid stepping on each other's toes. And beyond that, so do their bosses. I have personally had to deal with competing priorities from functional versus line management through most of my career (as no doubt did the people who worked for me!). This is where leadership and team working skills are vital (see later), underpinned with a common sense that we are all working together towards a common purpose and that all things can be resolved with dialogue and openness.

Just like the functional interface model described earlier, this matrix organisation structure will always be present, but what will change over time is which of the matrix dimensions are dominant. Sometimes the culture and structure of a business favours global over regional, and in this case, there will be a lot of control from central, with standardised processes rolled out across the business. Sometimes local or regional is dominant, and sites are left to decide much of their own ways of doing things with little interference from corporate headquarters. Sometimes global business units are present, managed as standalone businesses with little cross-collaboration. Whether your business is structured as global divisions or in regional geographies, will have a big effect on the decisions you choose to make, the key people you will need to influence and where you will need to be playing your politics.

You will also become aware that the structure of your organisation will inevitably change over time, as new CEO's come and go, and as new business strategies get deployed. This is inevitable and actually a necessity. Organisational structure must be a dynamic thing because your markets are constantly changing, so your organisation has to change to a form that better serves the markets as they shift. If your business structure does not change over time, this is a reflection that your business is too inward looking and not looking outward to your markets. Changes in organisational structure should be seen as a positive thing because it is the best way to better serve your customers. So my advice is always to embrace the organisational change, do not resist it. Out of change always comes lots of opportunities, so it is important to learn to go with it and not against it. To be successful in TTIP you need to understand that this matrix structure is a dynamic thing, you need to be aware of it and you need to work with it. It is always there, acting in parallel to your new product and new business development projects, and forms a key part of the environment within which you need to be working.

The Skillset Required and How to Lead

As we dig deeper into the process of TTIP, we can begin to appreciate how and why it is a long and complex process. And whilst an overall understanding of the process is important, coupled with strong leadership to guide the business throughout the process, what is also necessary is a varied range and blend of skills at different points throughout the process.

At the leadership level, important to success is having

individuals who can bridge the gap between R&D and the rest of the business, people who can talk on the same level as the technical experts, but who also have a deep appreciation of the way business works and who can keep the customer at the forefront of their minds. This individual would normally be the technical manager or director. But in my experience, such people with this blend of skills are rare, and once you get them, I suggest you hang onto them.

Transforming science and technology into saleable solutions for customers is a complex multi-step process, each step requiring a different skill set. During the early phases of the Phase Gate process, whilst the technology is being developed, part of the way down the innovation funnel, different technical skills will be required depending on the nature of the technology and technical complexity required. I split new technological products that we deliver to customers into 4 categories, each one level of complexity more than the previous one;

1) Technology Platforms – the most basic level of technology that can be exploited in a multitude of applications.
2) Products – a more refined version of the technology platform processed into a simple product form.
3) Solutions – low complexity products and designs that utilise the simple product forms.
4) Systems – higher complexity products and designs that utilise combinations of different solutions and simple products.

Each one builds off the previous one. You can't have a product without first having the technology platform on which it is based, you can't have the solutions without first having the product(s) that it utilises. To develop the more complex solutions and systems, you must first have the technology platform and/or product(s) available. This may already exist in your business, in which case your development project will essentially be a design challenge, bringing together existing products to produce a new functionality. Or, they may not yet exist, in which case your project will first need to develop the underlying technology required before developing the building blocks to be able to do the design phase. Some examples of real products and how they relate to Technology Platforms, Products, Solutions and Systems are shown in the table below. If you think about your own business, I am sure you can see how your technological solutions interrelate in this way, and how one feeds off the other.

New Product Types	Technology Platforms	Products	Solutions	Systems
Complexity	Basic	Simple	Low	High
Industries;				
Automotive	High Si - Al Alloys	Piston Head	Piston	IC Engine
Electronics	Semiconductors	Silicon Chip	Microprocessor	Laptop
Insulation	Ceramic Fibre	Fibre Blanket	Fibre Module	Furnace Lining
Technical Skills	Materials Science	Process Engineering	Applications Engineering	Applications Engineering

The practical result of this relationship is that when it comes to skilling up your team on a particular project, you will appreciate better that you will need a blend of appropriate skills to solve the technical challenges and deliver the required output. In the case of the examples above, developing the technology platform requires expertise in materials science, whereas, creating the product from the technology platform is actually a process engineering challenge, because the materials science already now exists and the challenge is about how to transform this into a different physical form. Beyond that, utilising the product in low complexity solutions or high complexity systems is more of a design challenge, which requires an application engineering approach.

From a wider organisational point of view, such analysis of the skillset required raises a broader question about the range of skills you have available in your organisation. For effective delivery of new technology to customers, the resources at each step of the pipeline need to be balanced, otherwise delivery will be bottlenecked. If you don't have access to enough Application Engineers to design the solutions and systems, then you're going to struggle to deliver such things to your customers, and if you don't have enough materials scientists you're going to struggle to deliver your technology platforms. If you don't have a particular skill set in-house for a project then you have two options, hire it in or out-source it. The latter can be a cost effective solution if it is a specialist skill only required for one project.

The skill set described above is a set of functional skills you will need to have in your team in order to develop the technology required, beyond that, to successfully take an idea right the way through to implementation you will need a fuller range of business skills at different stages, including new business development and sales skills, which we will discuss later in Chapter 5. But in order to make all of this happen, the overall most critical set of skills you will need for yourself is leadership. After all, you will be leading projects or project portfolios, or leading an R&D, technology or new business development department, and you will be leading people, some of whom will not be your direct reports. Leadership is probably the single most written about subject in the business world today. There are countless books you can read, seminars and courses you can attend. It seems that everywhere at every angle there are people offering to help you become a better leader. When I started in the world of business, the business language then was all about improving your management skills. At some point in the last 30 years this changed to leadership skills. And there is certainly a big difference in the approaches. When I started in my career, the business world still seemed to be populated by loud mouthed managers whose style was to shout people down, to humiliate them in public and to get one over on their colleagues. Fortunately the business world has evolved. EQ slowly overtook IQ and today's managers and leaders tend to behave in a more thoughtful, considered way. But that is not to say that you will not come across many people oriented barriers and challenges along your journey of TTIP. It's just that in today's business environment, the people barriers may be less overtly confrontational and more subtle in their style, which offers no less of a challenge to overcome, but requires a different approach to deal with. But have no fear, I will address these in Chapter 2.

Since guides to being a better leader are found everywhere in the business world, I do not intend to write an exhaustive Chapter on leadership skills, but below I have summarised the key points that I have learnt over the years about what makes a good leader. I love one page guides, I use them constantly, there are too many complex treatises on business subjects these days, for me, if you can't summarise it on one sheet of paper you won't absorb it and you won't remember it. So below serves as my one page guide to leadership skills. These are all the behaviours and attitudes you will need in order to motivate your team, particularly as your team will likely consist not only of your direct reports, but also indirects and people from other departments who bring the range of skills necessary to complete the project successfully. You will need all these skills in order to successfully take ideas through the process of Transforming Technology into Profit;

1) **Be positive** – you must constantly be positive about yourself and about the outcome of your work/project. You must display a 'Can Do' mind-set which you need to demonstrate and role model frequently. You need to get over the message to your team that 'we are going to do this, we will succeed'. You need to be positive and confident about yourself in order to give confidence to others.

2) **Be passionate** – exude passion about what you do, about your job, about your industry, about your field of expertise. If you don't care about it, no one else will.

3) **Be a listener** – you need to be a good listener and be seen to be receptive to other people's ideas. I have certainly found over the years, that as I rose in the corporate ranks, I had to come up with less and less of my own ideas, because my team already had so many bright ideas.

4) **Be trustworthy** – display integrity, be honest and trustworthy, and be seen as fair in your dealings with people. Don't display favouritism in the team, give everyone a voice.

5) **Be disciplined** – have a disciplined approach to your work and to the project/program. Make sure you have the necessary tools and methodologies to plan projects, to track progress, to communicate to the team. And constantly work with the team to improve and evolve those tools.

6) **Be controlled** – have a disciplined approach to

yourself. If you cannot control yourself, you will not be able to lead others.

7) **Have fun** with your team – get to know them personally, get to understand what makes them tick in and out of work. Go out to dinner with them, have a few beers with them, go and make a fool of yourself at karaoke together. 'Out of work' shared experiences are vital in creating a sense of team and belonging. Those who play together want to work together.

8) **Review frequently** and give feedback – for your direct reports, don't wait for the annual performance review or appraisal to discuss performance, talk to them frequently about how they are doing. For the team, have regular update meetings (the frequency will depend on the pace of the project and geographic spread of the team) on project and program progress. Communicate up and down the organisation to keep you, your team and your project on the business agenda. Receive feedback yourself during all these sessions and accept criticism positively, it will make you a better leader.

9) **Display vision** – you need to constantly put things into context for people, you must remind them of the big picture, of what they and you are working towards. This helps the team avoid going down blind alleys and spending too much time on things which might seem interesting to individuals, but which ultimately are non-value added exercises. This will help to keep things on track, and the subsequent good progress of the projects will help motivate the team.

10) **Be a role model** – Set good examples constantly, 'role model, role model, role model' all the

behaviours above.

To reduce the risk of successfully Transforming Technology into Profit in a medium to large corporation, you not only need to understand and know how to put into practice the process of innovation, but you also need to be working within an environment which has all the supporting structures and policies around you, such as a business strategy (see Chapter 2) and a new business development management system (see Chapter 6). If you don't, you will be putting your success increasingly at risk and relying more on elements of luck (which fortunately we all do have from time to time, so all is not lost). Not having some of these supporting elements will make your task harder, but not impossible, so it's important to focus on your own project and program tasks, and push on.

CHAPTER 2

BARRIERS TO TRANSFORMING TECHNOLOGY INTO PROFIT

Before we launch into the deep dive on each aspect of the process for Transforming Technology into Profit (TTIP) in subsequent chapters, I feel it is most important to document clearly up front the major challenges you will face in trying to implement your New Product Development process into your organisation. For me, this is the most important part of the book. Without understanding the barriers and how to attempt to overcome them, the rest of the 'how to' of your New Product Development process will just become a time wasting, resource draining, stress creating, box ticking, frustration generating exercise

To create, develop and nurture new ideas and transform them into successful new product launches, you will always be fighting on two fronts – externally (customers, the market, competitors, regulations, etc.) and internally (organisational structure, Not Invented Here Syndrome, and other potential blockers – see below). This chapter is about identifying and dealing with the internal barriers that you are likely to have to deal with. In the Introduction to this book, I introduced my 3Ps of business. For me, working within a business is all about handling 'People, Politics and Process,' and note that these are all internal aspects. There are many barriers you will face discussed in this chapter, and so I have tried to make some sense of them all by organising them under the three P headings, based on their predominant features. Not all are so cleanly categorised of course as they all essentially start with 'People' (that's why I put People first in my 3Ps) and focus on individual behaviours. 'Politics' is essentially about the interaction between people and the business culture this creates, while 'Process' is all the structure and mechanics that people put in place to try to make everything work.

Barriers Created by People

Lack of top management involvement – If the Executive team of your business is not involved in the process of innovation you are going to find it really difficult to make progress with TTIP. Creating the vision and desire for your business to develop new products has to come from the top if it is to succeed. There has to be someone who is the champion for TTIP at the most senior level in a business, someone who keeps this subject on the top table. Without an Executive champion, TTIP will not get onto Executive agendas, the projects will not get any air time, and they will not be considered important. Even having a CTO is not the whole answer, because the CEO has to buy into it as well. I once worked for a boss that had little interest in technology, even though our business strategy made it clear that it was central to our future. Technology and TTIP was always a shoe-in at the end of all our Executive agendas every time we met, so guess what happened? We never got to the technology agenda items, we ran out of time, so we never talked about the projects in open discussion. I had to do all my influencing informally outside of the Executive meetings. I had no opportunity to have formal buy in by the team as a group, which was a huge barrier to progress when formal approval items like Capex were required.

<u>Personal agendas</u> – People are people, and in any business there will always be individuals with personal agendas that create blockages in the progress of projects, for a whole number of reasons. Some of them are overt and some of them are hidden. Sometimes people do it deliberately to push towards their desired outcome, and sometimes people don't even know they are doing it, because they have been behaving in a certain way for so long. The latter type tend to have particular triggers, buttons that once pushed lead to repetitive actions. Much of this can be time wasting at best, but sometimes, it can be malicious and lead projects down the wrong path.

We used to have one senior director at Board meetings who came along basically because he was a friend of the Chairman, a total waste of time as he didn't contribute anything to discussions. The only time he spoke throughout the whole day, was whenever the subject of China came up as a potential new market for our business. Once his 'China' button was pushed, oh man, did he go off at a tangent and talk for hours. Not malicious, just time wasting. His personal agenda was clearly to give the impression that he was the China expert in our business. To keep things interesting for the rest of us, we used to have bets on the exact time in the meeting when he would start talking. We placed bets in 15 minute intervals throughout the 8 hour board meeting. Whoever had the closest time, won the pot and had to buy something with it that they would use at future meetings. Our rules were that we were not allowed to mention the word China, but boy could you try to manipulate the conversation in that direction. Great fun, certainly rewarding on one occasion when I won the bet (I won enough to buy myself a very nice watch), but what a waste of time for the business, though it was probably good for our own team building.

At the other end of the scale, in the same business, we had a Director who was a very clever guy, and he knew it. He was always the most intelligent person in the room, and during meetings, whenever he got bored, he would start to play games with people during their presentations, probing results, interpretations and progress to the n-th degree, twisting and turning conversations into needlessly uncomfortable confrontations, leaving young engineers downhearted and depressed, and sending projects backwards at times, all to prove he was the cleverest in the room.

As I say, business is all about People, Politics and Process, but the most important of these is People. To succeed in transforming ideas into technology and technology into products, it is critical to understand that the whole thing is a people driven process, the technology is the easy bit, we employ clever people to develop that, but it is people and their behaviour which is at the root of all the major challenges you will face along the way.

<u>Not invented here syndrome</u> – I first experienced the infamous 'Not Invented Here Syndrome' very early on in my career, when I was sent to one of our company's US

affiliates to work on developing some new technology and products with them. I was quite surprised as a young, naïve technologist to be confronted with negative attitudes by the local team. After all, surely we were working on the same team? It was only many years later, after I came back into contact with this same company much later on in my career, that I discovered that this US company had only been acquired by our parent company one year prior to me first arriving to work with them. It seemed obvious to me 20 years later, as a more experienced, mature individual, that the 'Not Invented Here' attitude I had encountered was a result of poor integration of the newly acquired company into the wider corporate business. These people did not feel part of the new Group that had just acquired them. They were probably worried about job security and the future of their site. They were no doubt proud of their expertise in their field and did not take kindly to some young newbie being sent over by their new corporate owners to show them how to do things. But I was not aware of any of these things when I first went there. My boss did not mention it before I went. No one thought to brief me.

How do you get over 'Not Invented Here Syndrome'? You first have to empathise with these people, and from that as a foundation, you need to get to know them on a personal level, you have to listen to them, to their ideas, to their complaints, just like being their manager in fact. You have to work to build a team effort and a team ethic on the project. If you come with new technology to be implemented at their site, you have to let them criticise it (and you must take it on the chin, don't take it personally) and you have to let them do some tweaking to 'improve' it, and at some point, when they've done enough 'tweaking' and 'putting it right', they will reach a tipping point, and suddenly it becomes 'theirs' and they will then own it and implement it. Job done! Once again, as with many of the barriers to innovation, this is about people, not about technology.

The stigma of 'technology' – People that work in the R&D department, or on the technology side of a business, are sometimes viewed as 'geeks', 'nerds' or 'white-coats' by individuals in other parts of the business. I have heard very senior colleagues, even quite recently, use these terms in board meetings in a very condescending way, as if these people are a joke, as if they are lower class employees. I have news for you. If you think this, then your business will never have successful new product launches. For technology based businesses, having the right depth of technical expertise is the absolute bedrock of the business.

The reason that these derogatory terms arise is that the personality traits of individuals who are technical experts generally lead to interpersonal behaviours associated with introversion. Introverts process things internally and thrive on detail, and so there is a lot of stuff going on inside their head, that's why they can be such good technical experts. These personality traits can also be associated with awkwardness in social situations, which means getting these type of people to work effectively with others in teams can be challenging.

I have observed on several occasions in businesses, several individuals who were extroverts (with behavioural traits that generally lead people into customer facing roles such as sales), clearly behaving and talking in some meetings, even at very senior levels, with the mind-set that being an extrovert is better than, and in somehow superior to, being an introvert and hence the use of insults like geek and nerd. Strange that this old-fashioned behaviour and ogance still exists, but I'm afraid it does.

There are certainly some stereotypes inherent in my short synopsis, and the reality is much more complex and nuanced of course, but this is a well-researched and widely published subject if you want to understand more about it. This is a situation where it really helps to have a technical manager that can talk both at the detailed level of the technical expert, but who also has the business credibility to be taken seriously by the rest of the organisation without such prejudices, as they form a very effective bridge between departments.

Much work has been done by behavioural psychologists on introversion versus extraversion and many other complex behavioural traits, with respect to behaviour and performance in the work place. Of particular help to industry has been the work on gaining a better understanding of how different personality types work together in teams (see Chapter 5). Analytical tools like The Belbin Team Inventory, The Myers-Briggs Type Indicator and a host of other psychometric tests, have proven very valuable in making people management a more accurate and sophisticated science when hiring new employees and building teams, rather than the gut-driven best guess exercise it used to be. Exposure to such tools and their value in organisations has been widely taught throughout business in the last few years, and so individuals generally have a better appreciation that different personality types are necessary for a successful business, that most people display aspects of both introversion and extraversion and that one is not necessarily better than another.

<u>The Idea Killer</u> – How many times have you heard this one, 'We tried that before and it didn't work.' What is this person's motivation? Genuine concern that the business is

going to waste time and money pursuing something that they know will not succeed? I think not. Embarrassment that some young upstart has suggested a potentially good idea and they haven't? More likely, and it's always going to be an older versus younger person scenario, because only an older person will have been in the business long enough to have 'tried it before'. And it's almost always an older 'technical' person, maybe a technical manager who has been in their position for 20+ years, who doesn't want to have his or her technical, guru-like knowledge and superiority challenged. I certainly experienced this memorable moment several times in the first couple of decades of my career. Can these people really not hear the words that are coming out of their mouth? Don't they realise how foolish they sound?

Whilst I have been guilty of creating a few of the barriers listed in this chapter myself early in my career (you only learn by making mistakes after all), for this one I can definitely say I have never dropped the 'idea killer' into a meeting. Now of course it may be true that the suggestion has been looked at before in one form or another in the past by the business, but of course the past is the past. Today can bring different people onto the problem, with different approaches and skills, different techniques, and there may be new technology around today that wasn't available 20 years ago when the idea was last worked on and didn't work. There may be very good reasons why it didn't work 20 years ago and they might be nothing to do with the idea or approach, it may have been a funding issue, an issue with higher priorities at the time or an issue with internal politics, none of which are anything to do with the idea itself. So if an idea was a good idea 20 years ago, it's probably still a good idea today and needs to be assessed against other options to solve a problem as if it's a fresh idea. I have also experienced a few occasions when technology we worked on was ahead of its time and the industry was not ready to make use of it, and some of these we resurrected 10, 15 or 20 years later. Also, if you're the project manager or leading the department, it is your duty as a leader to support and encourage your more junior members, not cut them off and make them feel inadequate. Also, if there is history on the subject that 20 years ago was not successful then that could give you a head start in terms of avoiding blind alleys and finding routes of attack with more likelihood of success. So please, never utter these words; 'We tried that before and it didn't work'.

<u>Technical Arrogance</u> – One self-inflicted barrier that can stifle progress on any project is Technical Arrogance. This is definitely one I will hold my hand up as guilty of in my formative years in industry. I figured that since I was the expert in the subject I was leading, then I should be able to talk about it at meetings and in presentations and everyone will listen surely. How wrong I was. I was also good at coming up with new ideas, so I would often pitch in with potential solutions to technical and operational problems at meetings. But what I learnt about human nature and behaviour over the years is that such suggestions need to be measured, timely and appropriate. People don't generally like an outsider coming into their business and telling them how to solve their problem (this is a version of the 'Not Invented Here Syndrome'), so the thing I had to learn most to try to overcome this trait, was to learn to be more humble. The arrogance thing used to come up quite regularly at my annual appraisal reviews with my bosses so it was definitely a real issue for me that reared its head in many situations; project meetings, departmental meetings, customer meetings, etc.

I remember one customer that I used to visit regularly in a technical support capacity over several years, where we used to have what I thought were really fruitful meetings, contributing great ideas to help improve their manufacturing processes. Not only trying to offer them better consumable products or develop improved bespoke new products, but also being involved in improving their operational efficiency and the costs surrounding the use of our products in their processes. I felt I was part of their team. One day, my boss (The President of our Group) visited them and he received feedback from the customer that I was 'technically arrogant'. I'd never heard this term before, but it sure stuck with me. At the time, it was a bit of a punch in the gut for me. Why would they say that? Because I had all the good ideas? I thought that was pretty unfair, I thought that was my job, that was why I was there, I thought I was part of the team. But what that feedback taught me is that it's not necessarily what you say, it's how you say it. There was nothing wrong with my ideas and suggestions, but maybe there were too many, and maybe I should have given the other people in the meeting more air time. Fortunately, this barrier is one that tends to diffuse with maturity and by climbing up the corporate ladder and gaining broader roles, because eventually you end up having to lead things which you are not the expert in, and you have to manage teams of experts (some of which may suffer from 'technical arrogance'). So watch out for this one, because the problem may be you.

R&D versus Technology – I have observed on numerous occasions in my career, a basic misunderstanding of what the R&D or technology department does in a business. I prefer to use the term 'Technology' as I feel it is a broader term which can cover a much wider set of activities. The term R&D tends to focus people on just the science and can conjure an image of people in white coats, standing in laboratories playing with test tubes. And this is partly where the stigma of the technology label can come from. The view by non-technical people in the business that those who deal in science are academic types, out of touch with the real world and not able to interact socially with others (see earlier in this chapter 'the stigma of technology'), people who just want to go into their laboratory and play with their science toys. I have discovered on several occasions in business situations where if I use Dr in front of my name, some people immediately have a stereotypical view of what a PhD type person is and treat me as if I'm some kind of weirdo (who knows, maybe they're right), so I have learnt to use Dr in some situations and to drop it in others depending on who you are with and what you are trying to achieve. It's definitely great for booking the best table at a restaurant.

I once had a boss who struggled badly with the R&D versus Technology issue and that created big problems for me and for the business. To him the two were exactly the same, and all he believed our technical staff did was pure R&D projects to develop new products. He just couldn't get his head around the fact that most of what the technical staff actually do is supporting existing sales and application engineering activities. I did an analysis of how the technical staff split their time between activities which were supporting sales of existing products, versus activities which were supporting the development of new products. The result was roughly 30% on new products and 70% existing products. Supporting existing products includes things like competitive product analysis, advising on product selection, product failure analysis, round robin testing around the group, some quality control work, and

IP support work. It depends how your business is structured, but in my experience these activities tend to be done by the technology department. Despite the 70:30 result, my boss still could not accept this, his view was that all the existing product work was done entirely within the sales team. This was a serious issue for me when it came to justifying what all our technology resources were doing when only 30 percent of them were actually doing the work he thought they were. Why aren't we developing new products faster? What's the delay? Well 70% of our resources are not developing new products! This 70% of work was not getting credited or properly budgeted. And this creates knock on issues when it comes to monitoring and reporting business metrics like % spend on R&D versus new product sales. If you're spending $1m on your R&D department every year, the chances are you are only getting $300k actually working towards new product development. Again, this is an important matter of putting things into perspective when it comes to making sound and well informed decisions within your business, about where to target resources against the direction you want your business to head.

Barriers Created by Politics

<u>Too much internal focus</u> – Many businesses I have worked in are very inward looking. They create so much internal structure, so many internal processes, so many layers of accountability, and have so many internal meetings, that people working in the organisations can lose sight that they actually have customers to service. Everyone seems to get wrapped up with the importance of their own job and with internal politics, and not pay enough attention to customers. This loses perspective for too many people in

businesses, especially those who never see customers face to face. This is a particular challenge for large, more complex, multi-site businesses.

People get so wrapped up in the internal culture of their own organisations, in personal power struggles, in one-upmanship in meetings, in the minutiae of form filling, that these things can become the most important aspects of their work day. Too often this internal focus creates so many barriers to making things happen, not just to your TTIP process, but to everything. This is also where the internal structure of your organisation can hinder your efforts to progress projects. The classic communication barriers created by Organisational Silos (different departments, different sites and different divisions) all serve to reinforce these internal barriers based around people, politics and process. Some internal focus is necessary of course. Building a strong culture, and great teamwork is very important for success, but it cannot be at the expense of putting customers first.

So first and foremost, you must talk to customers, get to know them and your markets. Too many companies have a lack of real understanding of their markets or are still basing their actions on out of date market information, you will see this in several of the later Chapters. Customers bring in the money to the business that pays your salary, pays your bonus, so put them first. Otherwise the internal will dominate the external in people's working day. This issue is really one of cultural versus structural balance.

The need for good, efficient management processes within a business is obvious, and the larger the business, the more complex is the organisation and the more process is necessary to stay in control. But every business needs to make sure that this is not done at the expense of customers. Customers and end users of your products and services must be the number one priority in everyone's job, even those that don't normally interact directly with customers. This is vital because it gives everyone perspective. If you put the customer first in everything you do, then you can begin to question all the politics that you are involved in, all the time sucking processes you have to do, and you can start to see them for the time wasting, non-value added activities that they are. This is where LEAN, Six Sigma, and other waste minimisation techniques, normally applied within manufacturing environments, can be useful approaches to analyse activities throughout the organisation and strip out the bullshit.

The culture of 'Technology' – The 'importance' and 'status' of technology in a business has a huge effect on how it is viewed by the management team and hence how it is prioritised as a business topic. In practical terms, this culture cascades down to manifest itself in the 'stigma of technology' for individuals and upwards in the 'lack of top management involvement'. It may be a consequence of how the business strategy is oriented and it is usually a consequence of the top management team not understanding or appreciating the role that technology plays in an industrial manufacturing business. You must have heard in businesses you have worked in when people complain 'this business is just run by the accountants'. I experienced this first hand in one of the first businesses I worked in as a technical manager. The finance director actually admitted to me one day that whenever we talked about technology projects at meetings, he found the subject very dry and boring. And hence it tended to get glossed over at meetings, paying lip service that it had appeared on the management agenda. This is a problem that runs two ways; is it his fault because the subject bored him? Or is it my fault because I didn't communicate it in an interesting and engaging enough way? But at least we got over the first hurdle of what the problem was, he openly admitted to me he found the subject boring.

This one takes a mutual appreciation of the situation and working openly together to support each other. This particular Finance Director left shortly afterwards (and went on to enjoy a long and rewarding career in less technically grounded businesses), before I really had the chance to educate him that technology is the lifeblood of industry, without it we would not enjoy the products we have today. Without it your business would not exist and without it, your business will not exist in the future. But we still need accountants of course to manage the cash flow, and all the debtors and creditors, otherwise we would quickly go out of business.

<u>Trying to do everything yourself</u> – Whilst it's true that technology is the lifeblood of any industrial business, that doesn't mean that you have to try to be the expert in all things and try to develop everything internally. This can be too big a demand on resources internally and can spread your resources too thinly, and you may find yourself lacking the key expertise required to progress a project because it is already in use elsewhere. When managing your technology portfolio, you need to consider external resources as well as internal. There are external partners you can work with to spread the load and the risk. This may be other businesses within your own group in other regions, it can be other technology groups within your company, e.g. a central R&D unit, or other businesses within the parent group portfolio. Beyond that, there may be university and research institutes that can share expertise and funding with you, though you will need a robust contract up front to

clarify IP ownership and commercial exploitation. The same is true when partnering with suppliers and/or customers. The latter is an excellent way to develop new technologies and products, as there is more likelihood that the product will be fit for purpose.

<u>Internal language/jargon</u> – The overuse of technical jargon within a business creates a barrier to understanding, which can block effective communication of the benefits of your products and technology throughout the organisation and especially to your customers. Every business I have worked in has developed its own unique language which has grown up over many years. Every day you hear people using acronyms and special terminology which is unique to the business, to the products, the technology and the manufacturing processes, so you will hear people talk about 'N135 mix' or 'ingotisation' or 'PQ department' or some other jargon. And every industry is guilty of this, whether your business is writing software, mining bauxite, designing medical devices, whatever, we are all guilty of it.

When you are a newcomer to any business this language of jargon is a real barrier to your integration into the business and it takes a lot of time before you soak up all the terminology, sometimes years. And if you actually stop and ask someone what N135 is, even some of the people who have been working there a long time and have been using the jargon for years don't actually know. How crazy is that? People normally start using the same 'jargon language' as everyone else in the business when they first join, so that they fit in and don't look stupid. 'What, you don't know what N135 is?'

I actually worked at one company that was based on quite a large site, and people used to talk about the various manufacturing departments by the codes that were used for the buildings they were housed in, e.g. PQ or PD or TP department, but get this, these buildings had been knocked down three years previously and the processes rehoused into a completely new building! Yet people were still talking about the manufacturing departments by these old, defunct building codes, can you believe it? As an outsider coming into a business, it is amazing how you can see things with fresh eyes as to how ludicrous they are. And it is a very valuable service you can bring to any business you join to speak up and stamp out such nonsense, it only serves to hold a company back.

Technical jargon is especially an issue when you are young and just starting and don't know any better. Fortunately, as you get older you realise this is all just nonsense and now if I hear jargon I don't understand I just stop and ask the person what it means. It is important to understand that this internal language is a significant barrier to TTIP, not only internally in terms of suppressing understanding within your business, but also externally, because people get so used to talking in this jargon that they actually use it when they visit customers! Why do you think your customer would know what N135 was, or even care? They have their own company internal language/jargon to handle, they don't need to be confused with yours as well. So my advice on all this internal language/jargon barrier is that you need to learn to talk in simple terms that everyone in the room will understand, if you have to use jargon, explain it clearly in layman's terms. Some people seem to think using technical jargon makes them somehow superior (i.e. the old 'knowledge is power' concept), but these days it just shows you up to be a poor communicator. Nowadays, I take every opportunity to try to stamp out the use of jargon in any business I work in.

Ivory Tower – Another classic barrier to successful New Product Development is the central R&D model (often these days called the Centre of Excellence). Without proper links to the rest of the organisation and to the markets your business serves, a central R&D department can become an 'ivory tower', lacking real understanding of customer needs (and how they change). When I took over responsibility for one standalone global R&D centre that was part of a multi-national group, I went round the rest of the organisation asking for feedback on how they viewed the R&D centre. Frequently I would hear the same criticism from sales people and business management, 'nothing has come out of there for years' or 'we haven't had any new products from them for years'. This feedback showed me that there was a widespread lack of understanding of what a central R&D resource is really there to do. It also demonstrated a proliferation of the widespread attitude that the rest of the organisation can just get on with their own jobs and sit back and wait for the R&D centre to come up with all the new products. This model guarantees under performance. The rest of the organisation has effectively cut off the R&D centre from the business and from the markets. Sat in isolation, the R&D centre will try to do what it can. The R&D team will work incredibly hard to develop new products, but without support from the rest of the business, and the market access that brings, it will struggle to make real progress and struggle to develop products fit for purpose.

The model of new product categories versus increasing technical complexity from Chapter 1 (Technology Platforms – Products – Solutions – Systems) is useful here in helping to understand the role of a central R&D facility in terms of TTIP. When you look at the skill set required to address each level of increasing technical complexity, it is easy to see that a central R&D facility is really there to deliver the underlying technology platforms. The new Products, Solutions and Systems should ideally come out of the businesses themselves, for a whole host of reasons. The bulk of the engineering skills needed to productionise new technologies and the commercial skills to commercialise new products will likely reside out in the business not in the R&D centre.

I dealt with this 'ivory tower' problem by instigating a Technology investment program and building a global network of Regional Application Hubs to link the R&D Centre to the businesses. The Application Hubs were more focused on the 'Products – Solutions – Systems' end of new product development and were skilled up appropriately. This provided a smooth transition of new ideas through the R&D Centre, through the Application Hubs, out to the regional businesses and on to their customers as new products. Giving the regional businesses more direct involvement in and ownership of new product development resulted in a more than doubling of % New Product Sales within 18 months.

Dumbing down your products – Always remember to focus on 'what it does, not what it is'. Some new technologies and new products may be quite 'sexy', like the latest new iPhone or Tesla, but many others are not. If your project is to design a new concrete formulation, you will know what I am talking about. The times I heard the phrase 'it's just dirt in a bag'. If your business dumbs down its own products in conversations, how will your customers ever believe in them? The 'it's just dirt in a bag' phrase is a great example of people dumbing down their own business' products, and creating a big barrier to selling not only new products, but also existing products. Yes, a new concrete looks more or less like any other concrete. It does not look even remotely interesting or sexy. But the materials science hidden within the formulation is extremely complex and what it can do can be of tremendous value. Your new concrete formulation may allow Civil Engineering customers to build a taller or longer bridge, spanning previously un-traversable valleys, opening up new trade routes and growing local economies. Or it may allow customers in the Petrochemical industry to line a new reaction vessel, running at higher process temperatures, and delivering new types of chemicals or improving process efficiencies and saving the industry billions of dollars – how massive is that! So never forget to focus on 'what it does, not what it is'.

Barriers Created by Process

Lack of a clear Business Strategy – If your business does not have a strategy, or if the strategy is too generic and woolly, then you're going to have a really tough time progressing any new technology and new product projects. If you don't have a clear strategy, how can you make meaningful decisions on which new opportunities to work on, how can you prioritise your new ideas list, how do you know which of the projects on your new business portfolio are the most critical for your business's success? How your business's growth and revenue targets are pitched has a tremendous influence on the nature of what new ideas and new technologies you will place your bets on and on what % of spending needs to go into R&D and new business development. Bigger growth scenarios usually mean higher R&D spend, riskier projects with bigger sales potential, and more acquisitions (some of which are likely to be acquisitions to bring new technologies in house). So there will be more riding on your shoulders if you're responsible for TTIP, which means more risk but more reward and a much more interesting time at work for the Technology and New Business development teams. Also, a business strategy should be cascaded down into all the departments and functions around your business in a way that is meaningful to them so they can be clear about what they have to do to contribute to achieving the overall business strategy. So for TTIP, this means that you should have a Technology Strategy that aligns fully with the overall Business Strategy. Your Technology Strategy will define the targets for new product and new business development that are required of the technology function to contribute to the overall targets of the business strategy, along with the KPIs to monitor them.

So if you find yourself in a situation where you have the responsibility to deliver new products and solutions to grow your business, but your business does not have a clear business strategy, then you need to put pressure on your colleagues and executives at every suitable opportunity to get together to prepare one. People often shy away from this because preparing a useful and meaningful strategy is a lot of work, is not easy to do and often needs to be facilitated by a 3rd party (usually a management consultancy), so can end up being an expensive exercise. But without it, you and your company will be drifting.

<u>Lack of market knowledge</u> – One business I worked at, used to regularly quote, internally and in its literature, that it was the global market leader in its main market segment, with around 40% market share. And it used to quote this all the time over the few years I spent there. This business had a long history and legacy of dominance in its industry, with a very strong brand. I recall tales of the 'good old days'

when the sales manager for Asia would rent a suite at the Peninsula hotel in Hong Kong, overlooking Victoria harbour, for a week and send out letters to all his Asia customers that he would be there between specific dates. The customers would make appointments with him and travel there to place their orders with him by hand. Those were the days! When I joined the business, the directors dining room had only recently been closed down, and I heard plenty of tales of daily boozy afternoon 'meetings', and their chauffeurs driving them home drunk. How business has changed in the last 30 years.

During my time in this business, there was a recognition that there was increasing competitor activity in the Far East, and a gradual shift in the market towards Asia, as Western customers moved their manufacturing facilities east. A few years after I had left, the then Managing Director decided to actually commission a new and independent market survey and discovered that the rise of competitors in India and China actually meant that their global market share had dropped to closer to 20%, and more than that, the company was probably not the market leader any more, with the next nearest global competitor, which used to be at around 30% market share versus our 40%, now estimated to be 22%. And all this had happened in less than 10 years.

This lack of market knowledge is not an unusual situation, and I have experienced it in several businesses in which I have worked, even in very large groups that have the resources to deal with it, and that actually employ marketing professionals. Strategic marketing is another poorly resourced and deployed skill in businesses. Many of the marketing roles and teams that I have experience of, generate large quantities of data, but seem to lack the skills, techniques or leadership guidance to do something useful with it. Businesses can generally keep their ear to the ground and gather information quite well (just ask any sales person for the latest market gossip), but unless you do something with that information, it is difficult to know how to make changes to your strategy to respond to changes in the market landscape.

The lesson here is do not sit on your laurels and expect that your business is still in the same position it has always enjoyed. Markets are changing faster these days, and your competitive position is going to change faster than you can believe imaginable, particularly if you are a Western business and do business in Asia. Unless you have lived and worked in Asia, it is impossible to appreciate the speed with which Chinese companies are launched and grow. There has been so much easy money around in the last couple of decades to fund state owned ventures and joint ventures and seed entrepreneurs, and even in the last couple of years, as access to money has become more restricted during the period of the government's anti-corruption campaign, access to funds still far exceeds that in the West. This is coupled with a culture that thrives on entrepreneurship. China has a whole generation of young educated adults that have grown up watching an endless stream of entrepreneurs and business people become mega-rich. They think it is their birth right.

So how does lack of market knowledge affect TTIP? If you do not understand basic information about your markets (market share, market sizing, market segmentation etc.), then it becomes impossible to reliably assess new opportunities for their potential revenue. And if you are basing your market numbers on old, out of date information, and if you are just best guessing, then the data you input into your project definitions and assessment criteria will simply be wrong. If this is endemic for all of your potential ideas and projects, then when you come to make informed judgements on project portfolio prioritisation, which projects to work on, which not, and which should have highest priority, then of course the outcome of your assessment will be wrong. When we fill in numbers in a spreadsheet, it seems to give people a warm, fuzzy feeling that we have captured the required information, job done and we can all move on. The fact that the data may be wrong or just a guess seems to pass them by. Often when preparing project definitions and assessing potential returns, the market data will not be perfect, and my approach has always been to put the best information we have in, but always with the proviso that it needs to be reviewed and validated. Almost all projects I work on need to have the underlying market data validated, and this always ends up as an action on the project team 'to do' list.

Another area in TTIP where the lack of market knowledge throws a massive spanner in the works is in preparing Technology Roadmaps (see Chapter 3 for more information). Overall, I am sure you can now see clearly what an impact a lack of market knowledge is going to have on your efforts to TTIP. Insufficient or ineffective customer contacts, not asking the right questions at customers, not taking a strategic marketing approach, not looking at the bigger market picture and not keeping up with competitive activity, will all impact your ability to pitch projects, to target projects, and to prioritise projects, and ultimately, even if you deliver a project to product launch, it is unlikely to deliver the sales return you expect.

<u>Trying to do too many projects</u> – This is a classic project management portfolio issue. This situation is created by 1) having too many people with a say in what's in the project

portfolio, all with their own pet projects they want to see worked on, 2) not having a robust process to filter ideas, so bad projects don't enter the pipeline in the first place, 3) not having robust phase gate go/no-go decision points and effective checklists, 4) being over ambitious about what is achievable given your business scale and resource. In particular, killing live projects is a very challenging thing to do, as people rarely want the responsibility of saying stop. I have been in many meetings where circular discussions on project kill decisions just go round and round and many times end up being deferred to the next meeting, in the hope that the project picks up, so a difficult kill decision can be avoided. Usually the project is being worked on because it was good enough to get into the pipeline, with a reasonable chance of success and worthwhile potential returns, but sometimes projects just don't progress as planned and can meet technical hurdles that become too time consuming and costly to persevere with, even with extra resources, all of which change the value proposition of the project to the business. Logic tells you that if you overstretch your resources you cannot focus on anything, and so if you try to do too many projects with too few resources you are unlikely to deliver any of them. Be brave and make a decision on what are your priority projects (refer to your strategy here) and what projects you really can resource effectively (make a case for hiring more resource if necessary). Delivering one or two big successes is better than keeping everyone busy on 50 projects and never delivering anything.

<u>Management tools that are too complex</u> – I have seen and worked with many management tools over the years. With respect to TTIP, these include Phase Gate checklists, project management tracker spreadsheets, financial

planning and return analysis spreadsheets, etc. What they all had in common was they were all very well put together, all very comprehensive, and all prepared by very clever people. However, it seemed apparent to me that some of these tools were prepared by someone sitting on their own in an office and then sending them out to the rest of the organisation untested (I know because I have been guilty of this in the past). If the authors had actually gone out and tried to use some of these tools themselves, or worked with the people that actually had to fill them in, they would soon discover, that in many cases, these tools were just too complex to truly be the help that they were designed to be. Some tools ask for information that is just not available or not easy to get hold of with any degree of accuracy. Some tools try to cover absolutely everything and their users spend far too much time filling in the forms. I get that every business needs, to some extent, to reinvent some of the classic tools to fit their particular business, I've done it myself a number of times, but my advice is that you must test your form, your spreadsheet, your checklist out in the business with actual users, to reconfirm which aspects of it are useful and which are superfluous. The danger is that project managers spend too much time filling in forms instead of actually progressing a project.

CHAPTER 3

IS IT A GOOD IDEA? – THE ART OF IDEA SELECTION

So, you need to develop new products for your business. Where are you going to start? How do you generate ideas and identify potential new business opportunities, either with potential now and/or for the future, how do you fill the funnel? How do you generate a list of ideas and develop them into potential projects and assess which ones are worthwhile for the business to resource? This is the start of the innovation funnel and is sometimes called the 'Fuzzy Front End' because you need to deal with many ideas coming from many different sources, all with a high degree of ambiguity and a lack of information associated with them.

Where do Ideas Come From?

I have worked in businesses where the CEO seemed to

expect that he could just sit back and the Technology team would come up with some ground-breaking, disruptive technology/product that was going to change the face of the industry and make massive profits for the business. After all, he employs all these white-coats to come up with ideas doesn't he? I have experienced this naivety first hand in Board meetings, and not just from the CEO, from several other senior functional heads. Everyone looks around at each other, expecting that someone around the table (not them of course) is going to come up with some world-changing idea that will grow the business meteorically. Such eureka moments do occur of course, but I've never seen one and I've never had one. If you're just one of the ordinary guys like me (and those sitting around the Board table with me), then you're going to have to do it the hard way. It has always puzzled me that people in business often seem to think that ideas for new products should come from the technologists. For me, technologists are the people that make the idea into reality, but the potential opportunity has to come from talking with your customers, understanding their needs, their challenges, understanding your markets and where they are headed. If you intend to branch out into new markets (check your business strategy!) then you're going to have to go out and visit new customers with the same approach and mind-set.

All of this is actually a business development challenge, not a technology one, and if you want to create a list of potential new product ideas, that's where you need to start. Unfortunately for a business, the type of people employed to do business development have a different blend of skills and behaviours to the ones required to work with customers to identify their needs on a practical basis. They tend to be more relationship focused and less detail oriented and often lack the technical skills to have a credible conversation with users of your products. Whilst, technologists tend to be the other way around. Quite a dilemma! My preference has been over the years to buddy up a sales or new business person with a technologist and send them into customers as a double act. Not only can you get relationship led and detail led conversations going on, to drill down into customer needs, but the new business development person learns from the technologist and vice versa. The role that in some cases covers both camps, and is truly in the best position to identify new opportunities, is the Application Engineer. In some organisations, Application Engineers are part of the sales team, in others, they are part of the Technology team. Whatever the reporting structure, the reality is that they have a foot in both camps, they understand enough of the technology to have credible detailed conversations with customers and also have enough of a sales driven approach to keep things commercial. So for me, the future is definitely in promoting more Application Engineering roles. I have found this the best way to address many of the challenges faced within TTIP. Though I have also found 'Application Engineer' to be a much misunderstood role, as the term is used to mean different things in different companies (in one US company I worked with, the Application Engineers were the people who drew up installation designs, like draftsmen), and so I have found it important to create a definition of what I mean by Application Engineer, so that everyone is on the same page.

My view of an Application Engineer is that the role is the expert in the practical use of a company's products, not in developing the company's products. In terms of the new product development process (as described in Chapter 1), an application engineer focuses primarily on delivering new solutions and systems, rather than on new technology platforms and products and so they have an important part to play in deploying technology at customers in new business development projects by acting as a bridge between customers, and your technology and engineering teams. In Chapter 1, I introduced the concept of the Application Engineering function. In line with this, an Application Engineer will be responsible for those activities that span the technology and sales and marketing interface, including non-standard product bespoking, new designs, product selection for customer applications, and designs with existing products.

One limitation I have observed in using either the Sales/Technologist double act or Application Engineer approach to generate potential new product opportunities is that because these people tend to visit customers to solve problems, advise on product use, help with installation, sell existing or new products, etc., their conversations tend to be in the present, so at best such visits only really identify opportunities they might have now, which can be quite specific to that customer. Whilst these may turn out to be good opportunities, particularly if you find the same opportunity is shared at several customers, the really big opportunities come from wider market trends rather than specific, individual customer needs, and turning the conversation towards that at a customer can be difficult. Firstly, because our people are not usually trained to think about the future and secondly, because the customer has probably never thought about his future needs also. So if you are going into a customer with a specific goal of generating new opportunities for the future, you need to go armed with a checklist of questions to help guide the conversation and the customer's thinking. This is particularly important when gaining information for

Technology Roadmap programs (see later in this Chapter).

And don't forget, before approaching customers to identify new opportunities, you need to prepare by referring to your business strategy (see Chapter 1) to give you some guidance about what markets to focus on, and hence which customers you should be talking to. This will also give you an indication of the size of new business pipeline you should be generating in order to achieve the growth targets (versus growth by selling more existing products and/or growth by acquisition) in the strategy, which in turn will give you some idea about how many and what size of potential opportunities you need to be generating.

Starting with your business strategy, understanding your markets and interacting with your customers must form the foundation of your idea generation to identify new business opportunities. But how you do this can come in many forms, and there are also multiple other directions from which ideas can and do come, all of which should be held up against the mirror of business strategy and market knowledge. Ideas can come from multiple channels;

Internal sources of ideas;
1) Internal Sales reports – distributing monthly summaries of sales reports can be an excellent way of sparking ideas in peoples' heads and promoting dialogue between those on the distribution list.
2) New business project and portfolio reviews – this is a helicopter view and internal review of what's going on in your new business development pipeline and new product development project portfolios.
    a. With technology based development activities, it is amazing how often there are multiple spin offs from one project into another and from one

project creating opportunities for several other projects. All great sources of seeking future possibilities but all need managing and holding up against the business strategy. It's easy to get carried away with such internal idea generation as it creates a lot of energy about what is possible in your business and is often the origin of people creating their own pet projects. I have worked in businesses where there is so much internal idea generation, so many opportunities, that it almost negated the need to go and talk to customers, because we already had more than enough ideas to keep us busy. This is a very dangerous situation to find yourself in.

b. Another benefit that can come out of helicopter view reviews is that you can see similar activities going on in different parts of your business, so you may have a team in China working on something that is similar to something being worked on by a team in South America. This way you can pool resources, compare notes, and usually extend your opportunity list. This is particularly easy to do when you have all your project portfolio on a CRM or other form of database (see Chapter 6).

3) Technology Roadmaps – these can come in several formats (see later in this Chapter) and are an excellent way to understand the trends happening in your market and generate potential opportunities from them.

4) Brainstorming events – these are usually focused on a certain topic (application, market, technical problem, etc.) and need good facilitation and process to produce useful output.

External sources of ideas;
5) Technology scanning – there is a lot of literature out there on your technical subjects and the markets you serve, but it can feel like a full time job keeping up with it all.
   a. At the start of my career, this was all about printed media; published journals and technical trade magazines. So the data sources were fewer but it took real effort to get hold of them. These days of course, with the internet, you don't have to leave your office to be connected to all the digital versions of technical journals, trade magazines, company websites, social media announcements, blogs, etc. It helps to set up alerts on your laptop to keep scanning for keyword subjects, but beyond this, it is still a very time consuming activity trying to keep up with all that goes on in your field.
   b. Another form of technology scanning that larger businesses attempt, is to hire a bunch of technical experts as a Technical Advisory Board for their business. This is good for gathering a group of relevant expertise in a room to focus on subjects of interest to your business, but it is quite difficult to manage, as the experts tend to be pretty out of touch with you as a business, so it takes time and talent to manage such a group to get effective output.
6) Intellectual Property scanning – IP scanning is a challenging and time consuming area.
   a. There are plenty of databases and services to go to that allow you to search IP databases regionally and globally for key words relevant to

your technology, applications, customers, competitors, etc., but this usually generates an enormous amount of data, hundreds or thousands of lists of patents, depending on how you target your keywords and how wide you want to cast your net. There is always the concern that if you don't have a broad approach, then you might miss something important. But a broad search gives you so much data that it becomes extremely difficult to do anything with it.

b. Another significant challenge with IP scanning is that patents are written in their own style of patent lawyer language, and sometimes in a way to avoid appearing on keyword searches, so you have to give a lot of thought to your search criteria. IP scanning is best done in a targeted way such that you generate a more handleable quantity of information. It helps these days that national patent laws are becoming increasingly joined up internationally with the Patent Cooperation Treaty (PCT), giving easier access to overseas patents, but in the end you still have the challenge of language anyway, if you want to see what is happening in China or Japan.

c. IP scanning is another classic situation where it is frequently given as a task to a junior person, or someone in a marketing role, neither of whom usually have the expertise in the target subject, such that these people come back armed with their search results and say, here you are, job done. But this is just part 1 of the job, the 2nd most important part is analysing these data, summarising and interpreting the information. This is a difficult task that takes a person very experienced in the subject to do effectively. Without this, your IP search can just be a waste of time. The whole subject of IP is covered in more depth in Chapter 4.

7) Market intelligence – discussions with market experts and reviews of published reports covering your target markets. Such information should feed into your Technology Roadmap program.

8) Trade shows/exhibitions – you'll never have so many potential contacts standing in the same room than at a trade show or conference, so work the floor.

9) Industry working groups – such as standards committees, conference organising committees or trade organisations, be they formal or informal networking organisations.

10) Competitive analysis/intelligence – there are multiple ways to keep up with what is going on with your competitors, such as web sites, announcements, booths at trade shows, market gossip, etc. But like many other large sources of data, these can just end up as a random pile of information thrown together in a company intranet. To me, this is only Part 1 of the task. Part 2, to make it useful to people, is to collate the data into a structured report with interpretation. This is often missing in a company because it is an 'and' job that nobody is tasked to do, but without it you will get little value from the gathering of the information in the first place.

11) Direct Contacts – including face to face conversations with customers, or via Email or phone calls.

12) Voice of Customer exercises – you should as a business be holding regular 'Voice of Customer'

exercises with key customers, as it allows you to get behind the random conversations and feedback that may or may not generate useful information and employ a managed approach to asking the questions you really want the answers to, for all aspects of doing business (not just their new product needs).

It is a huge amount of work to keep on top of all these sources of new ideas, and if you're on top of even a few of these, then you will likely be generating very long lists of potential ideas for new opportunities. But who should be doing all this work? Traditionally it is soaked up by lots of people in your organisation, in marketing or R&D departments, in a relatively uncoordinated way. But lately I have seen the rise of a new role in some organisations to try to handle many of these activities, a Technology Analyst (or sometimes called 'Innovation Engineer'). The technology analyst role is still developing in industry. I have seen it pitched as a very senior role with a highly paid, highly experienced person, and also as a very junior role for entry level graduates. My experience says it should be somewhere between the two. The problem with having a less experienced person is that they usually lack the capability and insight to be able to collate all the data and then, most importantly, interpret it in a way that is useful to the business and make recommendations. This after all is the whole point of these activities, to produce some useful output that shapes the direction of the business and new product development programs.

Personally, I have never really found it difficult to generate ideas in any business I have worked in. Lots of people have ideas in your organisation, if you only ask them, you just need to encourage them to speak up. They will usually be good ideas from something they've seen or spoken about at a customer, but it's usually a very specific idea. The task here is to find out if this idea is applicable to more than one customer, but normally the idea generator is not motivated to follow this up or contribute. They feel they have done their job by coming up with the idea and that it's someone else's job to do something with it. This is quite an issue to deal with as people can get disgruntled if you don't do something with their ideas or you prove there is no wider market for it and it doesn't get worked on. This can cause people to clam up as they feel it's not worth bothering coming up with more ideas because they never go anywhere. And this is not unrealistic, because most ideas do not make it to a project or to a new product, they get filtered out early on. This must be tackled by educating those involved in the process of TTIP, so they gain the perspective to appreciate where their idea fits into the process.

Assessing your Ideas

As I have stated previously, I have never worked in a business where we suffered with lack of ideas. What some of the businesses did suffer from however is knowing what to do with all these ideas once they had them. I have worked with a number of idea assessment methodologies over the years. What normally works best is to create a simple matrix of assessment criteria on a spreadsheet, against which to assess each idea. List all the ideas down the first column, and then evaluate each idea against these assessment criteria. Essentially, this takes the approach that to take an idea forward into the business, it will become a project, and so what you are really assessing with this method is the potential projects that the ideas would generate. Once you have all the ideas assessed, a simple ranking exercise will produce a prioritised list of ideas, allowing you to then focus on the top ideas/potential projects and take them forward to the next stage, and move down the innovation funnel. What the assessment criteria should be and what weighting you assign to each will depend on what is important to your business and relevant to your markets (refer to your business strategy), so there is no 'one size fits all' solution. However, there are several common assessment criteria that are routinely used. These can be categorised into three distinct groups as listed below, and so the spreadsheet layout should be organised to reflect this.

1) Strategic Assessment Criteria;
    a. Strategic Fit – a fundamental question to ask with every idea is, does it fit our business strategy? If the answer is no, it is very unlikely you need to spend any more time on the idea. A 'Yes/No' Dropbox is all that is required here.
    b. Ethics & EHS – as with the strategic fit question, if the idea cannot be clearly judged as ethical, or if it would take the business into areas where the safety or environment of its customers and consumers would be under any risk, then there is no point spending any more time on the idea. A 'Yes/No' Dropbox is sufficient.
    c. New or Me Too? – is the idea going to deliver something truly new to the market or is it going to meet a competitor head on? A Dropbox with 'New/Me Too' is suitable for this. In an industrial market, it is usual to be targeting the development of differentiated, unique products that deliver new functionality to a market, but it depends on your business strategy. Some

companies choose to make a fast buck through the Me Too route, but that is not within the intended scope of this book.
   d. Market need? – does the idea meet a current or future market need or is there currently no known market need? This category offers the chance to link your idea list assessment tool with your Technology Roadmaps (see later in this Chapter). If an idea has the potential to meet a market need identified in one of your Technology Roadmap sessions, then that is a big positive. If there is currently no know market need, then you would truly be stepping out into the unknown if you pursued such an idea, with a lot of market development required to make it work. A 'Yes/No' Dropbox is suitable.
   e. Potential Annual Sales Value – if the idea passes the initial fundamental strategic questions above, then the next most important question to ask is, what is the size of the prize if this goes all the way? Is the potential reward big enough to make it worthwhile doing the project? For this you will need to have at least some rudimentary idea of the overall size of the market you would be entering to be able to attempt an estimate. I have seen systems which request exact numbers in this category (including market size, sales potential and EBITA) and ultimately what people really want to know in this category is how much profit could it make? But without a detailed project plan, manufacturing costs and pricing information, without detailed market data, this is never going to be available at this very early stage. Deciding on the annual sales potential of an idea

that has to go all the way through project implementation (which may take 2 years) and through launch and sales ramp (which may take another 3 years or more) will always be a tough call to make. You need to call on your best market knowledge and make your best educated guess. No exact numbers are required, as this should be a 'Low, Medium, High' dropdown box selection. What low, medium or high mean in terms of potential sales value will depend on the scale of the target market and your market share. As an example, 'High' might be >$100m annual sales, 'Medium' might be $10-100m, and 'Low' might be <$10m, just scale it up or down by an order of magnitude to match the markets you are targeting.

2) Technical Assessment Criteria;
   a. Technical Capability – how capable is the business today in making this idea into reality? Does it have the necessary skills and resources to make it happen? Or would it need to outsource work to a 3rd party, find expert partners, hire new talent, etc. Typically this can be a low, medium, high dropdown box selection. 'High' meaning the business has all the necessary technical capabilities in-house to handle this idea, 'Medium' meaning it will need some outside support, 'Low' meaning it has very little or no in-house capability.
   b. Technology Protectability – is the technology that would have to be developed to make the idea real likely to be protectable by patent? A simple 'Yes/No' dropbox will suffice here. An idea that

is protectable is generally more favourable but a 'No' selection here is not a deal breaker.
   c. Technology Disruption Level – is the technology that would have to be developed to make the idea real truly disruptive in the market or is it just an evolution of existing technology? This can be a simple 'Yes/No' Dropbox. A truly disruptive technology can have huge advantages in terms of marketing your new product launch and delivering game changing functionality to customers.

3) Resource Assessment Criteria;
   a. Estimated Project Cost – this can be a tough judgement to make. If you haven't prepared a project plan and assessed resource requirements, how can you estimate the project cost (or timescale, or investment cost)? Assuming your ideas list is long (and typically it can be 100s of ideas long, even in a medium-sized business), then do you have the resource to prepare outline plans for each idea? Unlikely. So here you will need to make your best educated guess. Again, this should be a 'Low, Medium, High' dropdown box selection. What low, medium or high mean in terms of project cost will depend on the scale of your business and the markets you serve. The cost of your current R&D and new business development projects will serve as a good reference point. In a medium-sized multi-national business, 'High' might be >$10m, 'Medium' might be $1-10m, and 'Low' might be <$1m, just scale it up or down by an order of magnitude to match where your business plays.

b. Estimated Timescale to Complete – just as with the project cost estimate, deciding on the likely timescale to complete a potential project with no project plan is not easy. By completion, we mean the project reaching commercialisation (i.e. Phase 5 in the Phase Gate system – see Chapter 4). So again, this needs to be your best educated guess and should be a 'Short, Medium, Long' dropdown box selection. Typical gestation times for your current R&D and new business development projects will serve as a good reference point. 'Long' might be >2 years, 'Medium' might be 1-2 years, and 'Short' might be <1 year.

c. Estimated Investment Cost – is the project likely to require any capital expenditure to deliver the full sales potential? Will you need to build a new factory or a new production line to create capacity? A 'Low, Medium, High' dropdown box is all that is required. Refer to your recent capex investment history to scale your low, medium, high. In a medium-sized multi-national business, 'High' might be >$100m, 'Medium' might be $10-100m, and 'Low' might be <$10m, again, just scale it up or down by an order of magnitude to match where your business plays.

d. Access to market – this should be a simple 'Yes/No' Dropbox to assess whether the idea is targeted at our current markets where we already have good, well established routes in, or whether it is focused on a completely new market where we currently have no presence. The latter is not a deal breaker, but would certainly be a tougher challenge that would need additional resources and skills.

Many of the categories listed above require simple judgement on Yes/No or Low/Medium/High for all of the categories. There are no hard numbers required, and this is of course because at the embryonic stage for many of these ideas, there is lots of information that is not yet known or not known in sufficient detail to be accurate with. Putting a number in a spreadsheet is an easy way to fool yourself and others that you know the answer, when in fact it was just a best guess. It is therefore important to keep all this high level at this stage so you don't lock in data early on that come back to haunt you later. For a similar reason, it is best to limit the number of assessment criteria used. There are 12 criteria listed above, but to keep things practical, I normally limit my idea assessment process to a maximum of 10. More than that and the team can spend just too much time debating information which is not accurate or truly validated. The three distinct groups of assessment criteria are listed in a deliberate hierarchy;

1) Firstly, the Strategic criteria all serve to decide, even if it's a good idea, should the business really do this? If an idea can't pass the strategic criteria then there is no point going to the other assessment criteria.
2) Next, the Technology criteria all serve to decide, can we do it? Do we already have the capabilities or will we need to step beyond our core competences? In some systems I have worked with, I have seen this category rolled up into one single assessment criteria called 'Probability of Technical Success', but in my experience, one overall rating for this becomes over simplistic.
3) Finally, the Resource criteria all serve to assess, how

much effort will it take? To make the ideas into reality, is the business going to need to commit a huge investment or is it just a drop in the ocean? In some systems I have worked with, I have seen this category rolled up into one single assessment criteria called 'Probability of Commercial Success', but in my experience, one overall rating for this becomes over simplistic.

Another challenge with this process is who should evaluate the ideas? Who should make the judgements on each criteria and do the ranking? The technical manager? The business development lead? A Steering Committee? This is a risky area, as this suffers a lot from people thinking their own idea is the best or having their own pet project that they constantly push at every opportunity. So despite the analytical methodology of assessing ideas and potential projects, the influence of politics cannot be underestimated in this process. So what I have learnt here is not to over complicate the assessment process, otherwise you can fool yourself and others that the output is accurate. Again, this process relies heavily on having a good overall knowledge of the markets you serve and assigning assessment rankings and weightings dispassionately, both of which are extremely difficult to do with any degree of accuracy. My preference is always to share the burden and to set up an 'Innovation Council' in the business, to act as a Steering Committee with overall responsibility for the 'Ideas List'. The Innovation Council should be made up of the senior Commercial, Technical, Application and Marketing leads of the business as a minimum, plus other members to add breadth, depending on the scale and complexity of the business. It can also be useful to include some junior, up and coming employees from relevant roles, to add a different perspective and to ask the 'dumb' questions that really need asking. This also acts as a good training ground for young graduates and gives them exposure to the wider business and to senior executives.

Depending on scale and geographical split, you may also need to appoint an Innovation Council at the site, regional and global level to manage the different layers of ideation and project portfolios. Subject to your business culture, and how much it hands autonomy to the sites and regions, the sites are very likely to want some say in their own destiny and will therefore manage their own Ideas List and project portfolios. This should be encouraged, to foster participation in pooling all the Ideas Lists and project portfolios at the regional and global levels. This helps collaboration around your business and creates a mechanism to bounce ideas around the business beyond just the site level, often building small ideas into big ideas.

One of the most important tools you should have at your disposal when assessing your list of ideas is your business strategy. One of your assessment criteria should simply be, does this idea fit our strategy? Which is why it is the first question on the assessment criteria listed above. If your business does not have a strategy, or if the strategy is too generic and woolly, then you're going to have a tough time making meaningful decisions on your new ideas list and you will just need to concentrate on using your other assessment criteria and hope that the ranking lands in some way that aligns with the fuzzy strategy you have or with the general direction you collectively believe your business is heading. Such exercises often serve to highlight poor systems and methodology in other parts of the business. For example, Technology Roadmapping (see later in this Chapter) often highlights what poor market knowledge the company has. In the same way, assessing a new ideas list often highlights the lack of a clear, coherent business strategy.

Once you have completed the full assessment of all the ideas in your list, the next question is, how do you rank it to prioritise the list? Many people have put a lot of time into gathering all the new ideas and assessing them, so you want to get the maximum value out of your effort. You will see many different ways of achieving this in the literature. Some are based on financial calculations (e.g. Net Present Value (NPV), Internal Rate of Return (IRR), Cost Benefit Analysis (CBA)), some are based on commercial versus technical factors (i.e. market readiness versus ease of doing it), and some are based on the potential reward versus the difficulty and risk of doing it. Each will have their own calculation method, with formulae that use your assessment data to calculate an overall assessment value and then plot the results as charts or graphs. In deciding on your formula, your calculation needs to take into account that different assessment criteria may need different weighting in the calculation, depending on your business strategy, market dynamics and your attitude to risk. Deciding on your preferred method of ranking and on the formula you will use normally involves a lot of debate. You will find that many people will have strong opinions on what is right and the debate can get quite heated. My overall advice is 'keep it simple', don't get carried away with the intricacies of the process.

However, having done this many times in my career, what I have learnt is that all these approaches are mostly art rather than science. Just because you have some numbers in a spreadsheet and a formula, don't fool yourself that your calculation is going to come out with the perfect answer, it won't. Remember the quality of your input data; your numbers are usually best guesses, ratings are judgements. Again, look to your business strategy for guidance on where your business is heading, and select the appropriate tools to analyse your Ideas List data. Look at it from more than one angle, with 2 or 3 different methods and see what projects rise to the top. You will likely have a few big ones that look favourable no matter which way you cut the data.

Technology Roadmapping

One particularly useful technique to generate new ideas and opportunities, which has already been mentioned several times in this chapter, is Technology Roadmapping. If done correctly, I have found this to be one of the few techniques which adds meaningful structure to the process of gathering ideas. In addition, it acts as a useful focus to collate many existing ideas that are floating around in people's heads, but for which they never really have a forum to do anything with. Creating an Ideas List, as described earlier, is equally essential, but it tends to be a hotchpotch of ideas from myriad unconnected sources and can be a bit of a data dump, a focal point to hoover up all the ideas around the business. Technology Roadmapping, on the other hand, can be a powerful technique to focus ideas and link them to markets, and hence warrants a section in this Chapter to itself. Unfortunately, Technology Roadmapping is an often misunderstood and misused term because there are many types of Roadmap in use. Whilst they are all valid, and all have their use, many simply gather information together to summarise where current and planned R&D and new business development programs are heading, rather than truly trying to interpret the future.

One of the most basic types of Technology Roadmap serves to map out the evolution of a technology over time, looking back at the history of where it came from, how it got to where it is today and showing where it is heading into the future based on currently active or planned development projects, or hypothesizing about where it is heading in the future. An example of this type of Roadmap is shown below, which illustrates the evolution of semiconductor device manufacturing process "technology nodes" (i.e. minimum feature size) over time and shows the continuing trend for miniaturisation of semiconductor technology.

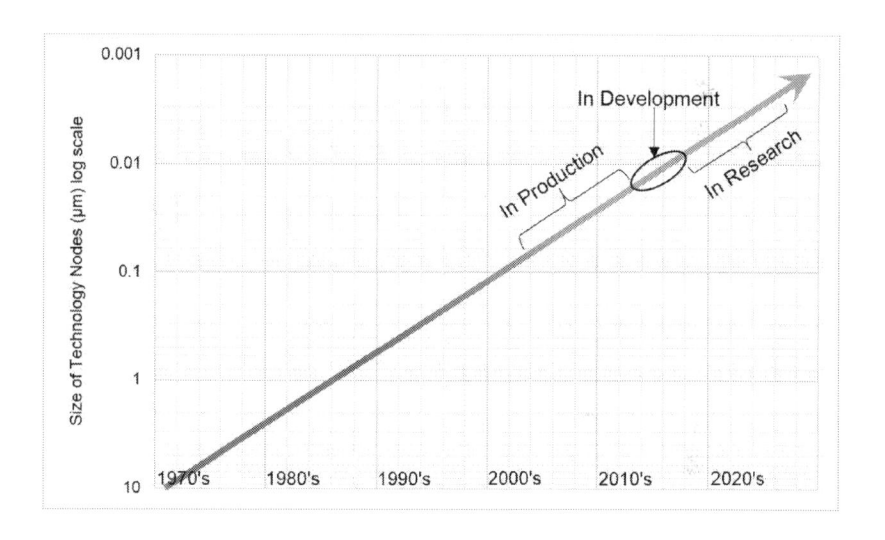

Some companies openly publish their Technology Roadmaps of this type to highlight to their suppliers what their future needs are. This is very useful information for a supplier, as it helps you orient your development portfolio towards the company's future needs, but since it is openly published, it is also open to your competition to see. Trade organisations (e.g. the semiconductor industry association) and government trade bodies also sometimes publish Technology Roadmaps of this sort, from the point of view of a particular market, which is again useful for businesses servicing the sector.

These type of Technology Roadmaps are useful communication tools, both internally and externally for a business, indicating the direction of travel for the technology that underpins a particular market and mapping out the future. But more useful for a business internally, are the types of Roadmaps which dig deeper and build on such information (whether openly published as above or generated internally from market knowledge) and link market trends to technology needs and the resources needed to deliver on them. These types of Roadmaps also come in various formats, but can get increasingly complex (e.g. as illustrated below), depending on the level of information you want to include.

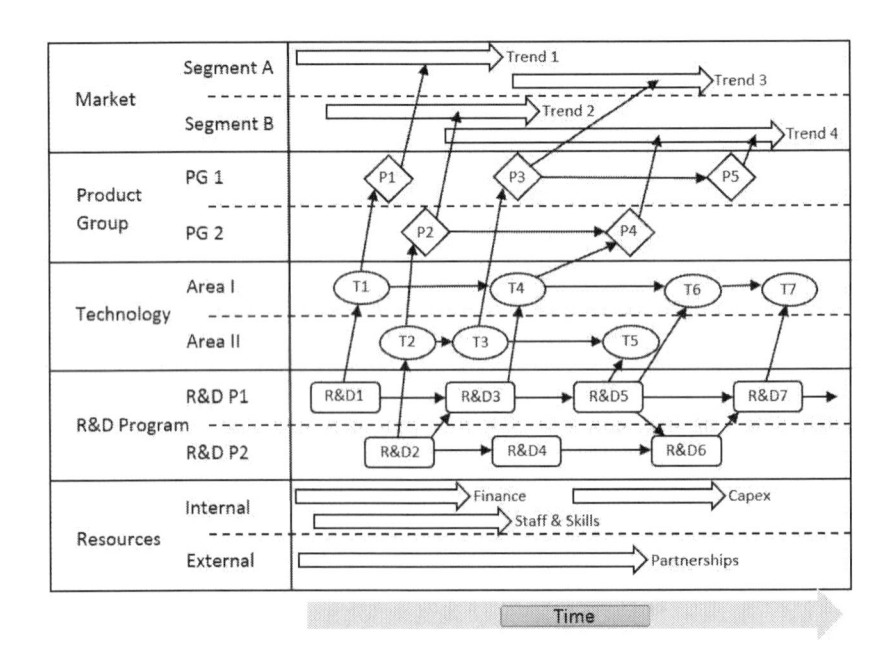

Market-Led Technology Roadmap (MTR)

The type of Technology Roadmap that I have found most

effective for identifying opportunities, and hence leading to real projects, is a Market-led Technology Roadmap (MTR). This type of Roadmap serves to identify the trends in the markets you are focused on and helps to prepare and position your business ready to profit from them in the future. This is essentially crystal ball gazing. This market-led Technology Roadmap identifies future opportunities by first analysing the target market segment dynamics and then understanding the related market trends and their drivers. This technique helps to identify and prioritise those R&D projects that your business should be starting to work on now in order to meet these future demands. You will then be in a good position to put in place the appropriate technology, capabilities, skills and partnerships that are needed to deliver the new technologies and products required to meet these future customer needs.

Over the last few years of running market-led Technology Roadmap programs globally, I learnt a lot about how to run a good Roadmap session, about what worked and what didn't. What I discovered was that there are 6 key elements that need to be in place to deliver good quality output;

1) Scope – Is the Market segment selected for the Roadmap the right one? Do we have sufficient knowledge in the business and the assigned team for a rich and fruitful discussion? Are we clear on the boundaries of the market (i.e. what will we not include in our discussions)?
2) Ownership – The Roadmap has to be owned by the person with market responsibility (usually a product manager), not by the Technology person, otherwise it will be viewed as an internal Technology exercise rather than an external, market facing exercise. This

is where modifying the name of the process from Technology Roadmap to Market-led Technology Roadmap helps.
3) Facilitation – it is critical to use someone who is experienced in the Roadmapping process to keep the team on task and keep the process moving smoothly.
4) Preparation – it is important that the initial market segmentation work is done before the actual Roadmap event, otherwise the Roadmap discussion gets bogged down in debating the market data (or rather the lack of it) instead of focusing on market trends and drivers.
5) Team mix – you need to make sure that you select colleagues with sufficient depth and breadth of knowledge to cover the target subject for your Roadmap team, with a mix a functions present (Technical, Commercial, Applications, etc.). I have found 20 people is around optimum.
6) An independent 'expert' – to enhance the richness and relevance of your Roadmap discussions and maximise the quality of their output, the most important ingredient is to add an independent point of view to your team. There are five options, in decreasing order of preference;
   a. Customers – the single best thing you can do to improve your roadmap session is to include customers in the process, and I really would not advise holding a Roadmap session without direct customer input.
   b. A consultant relevant to the industry – a consultant can add broad market perspective and should be relatively unbiased, but they are expensive to hire and often it is not at all easy to find someone who works in your particular

chosen market.
c. An academic that works in this area – a relevant academic may lack some of the market perspective, but at least they should be able to bring some industry contacts to the discussion for useful follow up.
d. A Technical or Marketing Director from another part of your business – can provide an effective sanity check.
e. A suitably knowledgeable and outspoken Rebel from within your business to challenge the team – it is always good to stir up the discussion, to have someone who is prepared to ask the obvious and sometimes awkward questions.

When it comes to the actual recording of the discussion at a Technology Roadmap event and the output, a simple spreadsheet is all that is necessary to lead the team through the discussion, capture the data, and produce a useful output. All the data capture should be via free form text in each cell, no preselected dropdown boxes, to accommodate the market data and the free flowing nature of the Roadmap discussions.

The very first thing to do with the team, is to be very clear and concise with nominating the market you are focusing on for the Roadmap session. Use language that everyone understands and check with the team that they have a shared understanding of what you are all working on before launching into the market data capture. For example, you need to state clearly the geographic boundary of the market, is it global? Is it Asia? Is it China? This makes a huge difference to the market data you complete. My experience is that the whole process works best if you choose a specific market, rather than a broad market, but a market that is still big enough and complex enough to have a range of trends to debate. It cannot be too big or too small. If you choose a big market, then there are just too many different complex segments, each with many market trends, and you will struggle to make any meaningful progress with it. If you choose a market that is too small, then the debate becomes very narrow, reflecting few key market trends. Some examples to illustrate this point are listed in the table below.

Broad Market	Specific Market	Geography	Roadmap focus
Iron & Steel	-	Global	Too broad
Iron & Steel	Galvanizing Lines	Global	Broad, but possible
Iron & Steel	Galvanizing Lines	Asia	Just right
Iron & Steel	Galvanizing Lines	Vietnam	Too narrow

In terms of shared understanding, remember that the market you nominate is in terms of what it means to you as a business. For the example above, 'Galvanizing Lines' will mean something completely difference if you are an EPC business supplying complete galvanizing lines, compared to a consumable supplier of special lubricants for galvanizing lines, the scale of these two markets will be vastly different and the specific trends and technology drivers will also be vastly different. The Roadmap always has to be approached in the context of what the market means to your business. Do not try to go outside this boundary or you will get severely side-tracked. Once you have decided on your specific market, write it clearly at the top of the Roadmap as the title of the document, e.g. Iron & Steel – Galvanizing Lines – Asia, so it is always there as a constant reminder during the process.

Now you can start to complete the Roadmap spreadsheet. This captures information under three main sections, with sub-headings, each of which should form a column on the spreadsheet;

1) Market Segmentation;
   a. Market Segments – populate column 1 with all the sub-markets which segment the market you have selected. Typically there will be between 3 and 7, but it can be as many as 10 or more. If you end up with more than 10, then it suggests your choice of market is still too broad and you should consider refocusing, otherwise you may complicate and confuse the whole Roadmap process. How you choose to segment your chosen market largely depends on how your business addresses that market, e.g. with the earlier example of 'Iron & Steel – Galvanizing Lines – Asia', you may choose to segment by geography and list all the countries in Asia that have an active market in this area, alternatively you may choose to segment by process or technology, e.g. there may be several different designs of Galvanizing Line in the market, so you may choose to segment by Design 1, Design 2, Design 3, etc. Once you have identified clearly each market segment, you can then move on to capturing the relevant key market data for each, and this is where the fun starts.
   b. Market Share (%) – what is your business's current % market share in each of your market segments? Remember to consider the geography of the market you have chosen.
   c. CAGR (%) – Compound Annual Growth Rate – what is the growth rate in each of your market segments?
   d. Market Available – what is the current total size

of each of your market segments? Use currency relevant to the geography you have selected, and always state it clearly in the spreadsheet.

If you have never been involved in one of these market-led Technology Roadmap events, you would be forgiven for thinking that the market segmentation information would be the easiest to complete. After all, you have selected a clear market, and identified all the relevant market segments, all you have to do is note down the simple market data (market share, CAGR, market size). What could be difficult about that? Having personally led dozens of Technology Roadmap events, and facilitated dozens more, what I learnt very quickly is that, if not managed effectively, this can turn out to be the most difficult and time consuming part of the whole process. Why? Because these early discussions during the Roadmapping process quickly highlight the lack of real market data that businesses actually have. They have plenty of anecdotal information, old market data and lots of people in the business have useful experience and plenty of opinions, but when it comes to real, hard, up to date information that everyone agrees with and can commit to, that, in my experience, is severely lacking in many businesses. Some of my earliest Roadmap events would spend up to 80% of the time trying to complete the market segmentation data, leaving very little time for the actual Roadmap debate of trends and drivers. This is why I learnt to add in a pre-session to more effectively and painlessly gather the market data, so that it did not distract from the main event. There are two levels of data required, first are the high level numbers for the overall market that you have chosen, and next will be these numbers broken down by market segment. So for the example used above, your

Roadmap document might start to look something like this;

Market; Iron & Steel – Galvanizing Lines – Asia Company; EPC turnkey supplier of complete galvanizing lines Market Data; 30% overall market share, 3% CAGR, $500m total market size			
Market Segments	% Market Share	% CAGR	Market Size ($)
Line Design 1	45	1	200
Line Design 2	25	3	100
Line Design 3	20	4	150
Line Design 4	10	10	50

Please note that these are completely fictitious numbers I have made up purely for the purposes of an example and to illustrate a point. The point being, why do you need all this data up front? Why not just start debating the trends and drivers and get to the point of the Roadmap exercise? The reason is, that you need to make sure that the debates you have and conclusions you reach are all grounded in market reality, so that you can make decisions which are truly directed at growing your business, otherwise you can end up discovering some interesting trends and identifying some great projects, but they may not make you any money. In the example above, the business has a large market share in Line Design 1, but at 1% CAGR this is clearly a declining market, so should you be putting any effort into developing new technologies to service this business? Or should you just continue to service it with existing solutions? On the flip side, Line Design 4 is clearly the up and coming new design on the market, with 10% CAGR, plus the business only has a small market share, so there is plenty of room for growth. The subsequent debate on trends will inevitably start to capture some of these market dynamics and lead to some real practical conclusions for development projects that the business should start. And you can be safe in the knowledge that these will be addressing a real growth market segment, because you have already done your marketing homework. Without the market data, your Roadmap will just be adding a long list of ideas to your already very long 'Ideas List', making selection and prioritisation a more challenging task.

2) Trends and Drivers – this is the core of the Roadmap;
   a. Market Trend – in what direction is the chosen market segment heading in the future? What is the market trying to achieve? What are the goals and targets it aspires to? This is where the debate really begins.
      i. If you have selected your team appropriately there will be plenty of good quality input at this stage, with many thoughts, ideas and suggestions being aired. This is the most important part of the whole process and where facilitation is critical to avoid mission creep. Ideally you should get the team thinking of trends that will impact the market in the 3-5 year timescale to keep things relevant and practical, but inevitably some trends emerge that are affecting the market now or sooner than 3 years, and some trends are likely to be much longer term. The timescale is all captured later in the process.
      ii. Of the many Technology Roadmap events I have led over the years, in every one of those sessions, I have observed that there are only 5 categories of market trends. All the trends that your team suggests will fit into one or more of these 5 categories. Typically your customers are looking now and in the future to 1) improve their product or process safety,

2) improve their product or process performance, 3) improve their process cost effectiveness, 4) lower their direct process cost, and/or 5) meet new or upcoming market regulations. In Chapter 7, you will see that these same 5 categories mirror the 5 categories of new product benefits that should be the focus of marketing any new product. Check out Chapter 7 for further useful background on these 5 categories, as they will help you make sense, and add some structure into your Roadmap document, when you are recording the trends. The 5 categories are also really useful to know because they can be used as prompts if the debate gets stale and the team runs out of ideas. For example, if no one has mentioned any trends relating to market regulations yet, then as the lead, you can challenge the team to think about whether there are any up and coming, or changing, regulations that are going to affect the market over the coming years.

b. Technology Driver – what new technologies does the market segment need in order to achieve the goals and targets in the trends? You should interpret this in the context of your own business, products and technologies to keep your answers relevant. We call this section 'Technology Drivers' because these new technologies will 'drive' the market trends. Without these new technologies being developed, the market trend cannot be achieved. For each trend you have recorded in the previous column, you should debate with the team what are the technological barriers to delivering the trend, and what might your business offer to make this happen.

3) Output;
   a. Project – what projects does your business need to execute in order to develop the new technologies and products identified in the Technology Driver section? Once you have populated your list of market trends and their associated technology drivers for each market segment, you can then launch into suggesting some projects that you might actually do. This is where the debate gets practical and this is the bit that most people love, because most of the people in your team will be engineers of one sort or another and will be much more comfortable with focusing on a problem rather than talking broadly around a subject. It is a constant challenge throughout the Roadmap process to rein these individuals in, because they are always wanting to jump to the end of the process and start talking about how they would approach a particular technical challenge raised in the debate. Here you should record no more than the bare outline of what the project needs to achieve, what new technology or product it needs to deliver, and not dive into so much detail that the team starts planning the project. That is for the next stage if the project gets selected for further work.
   b. Year opportunity becomes commercially significant – for each market trend/technology driver combination, what year will the technology

driver become a significant commercial opportunity? This basically asks the question, when do we need to be ready to sell our new product to the market? Knowing this allows you to work back with a rough project timeline and determine when you should be starting the project. If a trend is such that it will not present a commercial opportunity for 5 years' time, and it is going to take your business 3 years to develop and commercialise it, then there is no urgency to start the project immediately, but you should build it into your R&D program for the next year or two. You will always find in Roadmapping events that the debate raises technology drivers that are needed now, not just in the future. Your business may already be working on these and so you should record them in the project list against the current year to link the Roadmap document to live projects, but you may also identify current drivers that you are not currently working towards. So some potential projects may be identified that have a need for urgency.

c. Comments – this is just a catch all column in case there are important notes that the team wish to capture on a particular trend/driver/project combination that are not easily recorded in the rest of the spreadsheet.

The MTR process described above, and the approach to capturing the data and discussions, has been refined over several years through leading many, many Roadmap sessions. Another key thing I came to understand over time, was that the Roadmap process is not just one single session. As a process, there are three steps needed to produce a meaningful and useful Technology Roadmap;

1) Market Segmentation Preparation – as described earlier, it is important to separate the market data gathering and the trends/drivers discussion, because gathering the market data is usually a challenging task that sucks up session time. I suggest holding the market segmentation meeting with the full team a few weeks before the main Roadmap session. This is where the input from the independent, external market expert is most valuable, as you often find that your own knowledge of customers, markets and trends is lacking. The Roadmap owner should take the lead and the facilitator should record the information into the Roadmap spreadsheet. This type of session can be a virtual event over Skype, but often a follow up session is required to review and finalise the market data with the team before launching into the next step.

2) Debate the Market Trends & Technology Drivers – this should absolutely be a face to face session to facilitate the discussion. Virtual meetings are rarely effective, as they tend to suppress participation. This session is where an independent 'sounding board' is most useful in challenging and shaping the discussion, to avoid what my good friend and colleague Robin Mottram once described to me as the 'echo chamber effect' of the same voices producing the same output. This is because the reality in any business is that you tend to bring the same people out every time to cover the same topics. There are only so many people in your business with the necessary expertise in specific markets. Once you have worked through the trends/drivers, there will

always be some need for tidying up the spreadsheet, as the recording of the discussion on the day always ends up with a whole bunch of distorted, scrappy notes that need further reflection and refinement. This should be done by the facilitator straight after the session.

3) Review of Roadmap output – to finalise the Roadmap process, the Roadmap Owner, facilitator and senior Technology team should review the completed Roadmap spreadsheet, run through the projects identified and prioritize them based on the information available in the Roadmap document. The selected potential projects should have an owner assigned to each, who is responsible for preparing an outline project proposal (see Chapter 4). All proposals then go forward to the 'Ideas List' to be assessed alongside the other potential ideas/projects from other sources. This review of the Roadmap output can be a virtual session over Skype. My experience with potential projects that come from the Roadmap process, is that since these are already well developed and well-grounded in real market needs, they are the most likely to be selected during the Ideas List assessment to go forward to Phase 1 in the Phase Gate process (depending on the Year the Opportunity becomes commercially significant), preparing the Project Definition. This is when the project gets a project leader and a team assigned and project planning begins.

Experience has shown me that trying to squeeze these three sessions together into one single Roadmap event can be a very frustrating experience. Two things can typically happen if you try to do it all in one event. Firstly, as explained previously, the meeting soon unearths a distinct lack of real market knowledge and data to fill out the market segmentation side of the spreadsheet. Secondly, if you send out the spreadsheet beforehand, on the day you have the session, the relevant business leader has sometimes already completed it. But they have obviously done it by starting from the right hand side, by filling in all the projects the business is doing right now and working backwards to justify why they are doing them with the relevant market trends & drivers. This is a complete waste of the power of the Roadmap process, highlights zero new opportunities, and is a massive waste of time. I first observed this behaviour the very first time I tried to use this technique in a small business in Australia. One particular challenge is that a business usually serves multiple markets, so a Roadmap session that tries to cover a whole business can get into a real mess. That's why I learnt to focus on targeted markets.

If there is not sufficient preparation, and if the process is not facilitated by someone who knows the roadmap process inside out and how to keep people involved and engaged, it can be a real time waster. One danger to watch out for is that you can get individuals who seek to highjack the process to air their particular bug bears, grievances or ideas on a whole bunch of topics, trying to solve the problems of the whole business, so it's important to keep the session on track and focus all discussion on the market segment only.

Effective Roadmapping requires a big commitment of resource, it is not to be started lightly. Those involved need to understand why they are involved, what the purpose of the process is, and why it is a valuable use of their time. And once complete, follow up is essential, with regular communication to keep people involved and keep the information relevant. Remember, the Roadmap you prepare now is only relevant to market trends that exist today. To keep it relevant, you will need to challenge the roadmap regularly. The frequency of this will depend on your market and the resources you can apply, but generally once a year is a good rule of thumb. The question then becomes, do you just do a quick review of what you did last year or do you start from scratch. The quick review scenario runs the risk of missing new things in the market, which could potentially reduce the effectiveness and accuracy of your roadmap over time.

One suggestion in the Roadmapping rules above is to include customers in your Roadmap session. As you get better at Roadmapping (and it takes a lot of practice, it may take 2 or 3 years before your organisation is effective at Roadmapping and not just going through the motions), the next step is that you should be persuading your big customers to share their Roadmaps with you to ensure alignment of what you are doing with where they are heading. The ultimate position (and when you know you are truly partnering with your customers), is if they invite you to take part in preparing their Roadmaps.

Overall management of the company's Technology Roadmap program should sit with the Innovation Council (see earlier). How many Roadmap sessions you organise each year will depend on your business strategy and the number of different markets and market segments that you serve or plan to serve.

So what happens next with the Roadmap document? The potential projects the team identified have gone forward into the 'Ideas List' and the most urgent ones have likely been prioritised and selected to start work on, so it has proven itself to be a valuable process for your business. But what about the Roadmap itself? Your roadmap document will at this stage be a list of technology, R&D and New Business development projects, cross referenced against timescales of when they need to be completed by, to be ready to service the future market needs of customers. With some opportunities, you will inevitably find that you actually have the technology available now to address the opportunity and the market need is immediate, so this becomes an application engineering project rather than an R&D project. These projects all need to be individually assessed and validated, by preparing an outline project proposal for each, submitting via the 'Ideas List', and put into the pot of potential projects for assessment and funding by the business. It is an important concept to appreciate that you don't need to start all the projects you identify straight away, some will not be needed for 4, 5 or more years, and so you may not need to start the projects until next year or the year after.

With respect to the Roadmap document, you will note that the Technology Roadmap examples earlier are published in the form of charts, whereas the output of our market-led Roadmap session is a spreadsheet. This is because the methodical process of the market-led Roadmap produces far too rich a data set to dump directly into a chart. Almost all Technology Roadmaps published in the public domain are in the form of charts, and so there is a natural tendency for people to follow similar formats, but I have found this to be a mistake. A chart cannot lead the team through the multi-step process effectively. I have witnessed people try to record Technology Roadmap discussions directly into a chart format, but in my experience, this approach inevitably fails to capture much of the good quality output from the debate and leads to an overly complex, difficult to follow Roadmap chart. This approach is essentially just an attempt to shortcut the process of Roadmapping and is not recommended. So the Roadmap document that really matters is the final spreadsheet, the chart format is important, but should be viewed simply as a communication tool to produce a simple overview of the Roadmap that helps with articulating the output.

I have developed several formats of visualisation charts over the years, as these are useful for explaining your vision for the future in presentations, reports, etc., but I have learnt to keep them relatively simple, otherwise there can be just too much information displayed, leading to data overload for an audience. The visualisation chart can be prepared at the market or market segment level, depending on the number of segments and trends that need to be displayed, but normally the market segment level has more than enough data to fill the chart without getting overloaded. Below is an example using the market segment from earlier in the Chapter. As with the market data, the market trends are just made up for the chart.

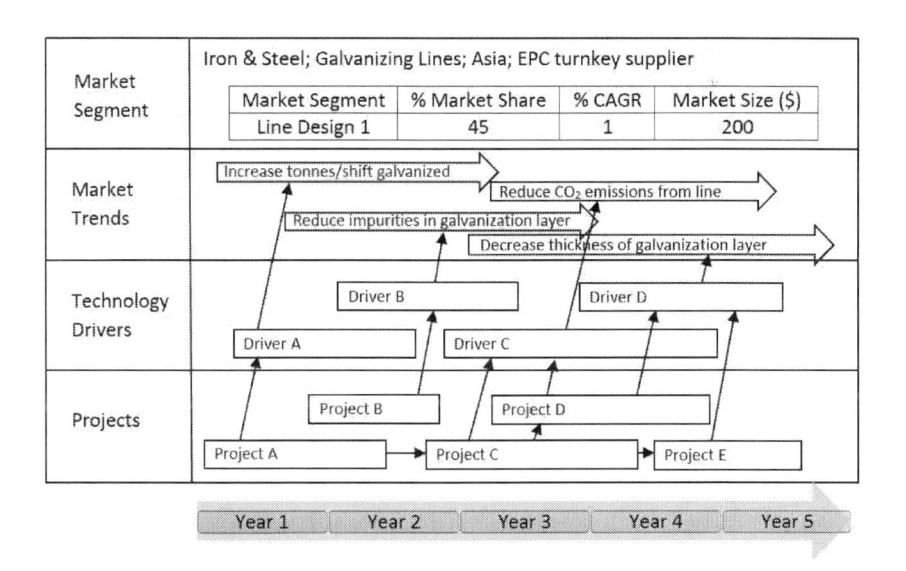

Market Segment	Iron & Steel; Galvanizing Lines; Asia; EPC turnkey supplier			
	Market Segment	% Market Share	% CAGR	Market Size ($)
	Line Design 1	45	1	200

Market Trends:
- Increase tonnes/shift galvanized
- Reduce impurities in galvanization layer
- Reduce CO_2 emissions from line
- Decrease thickness of galvanization layer

Technology Drivers: Driver A, Driver B, Driver C, Driver D

Projects: Project A, Project B, Project C, Project D, Project E

Year 1 — Year 2 — Year 3 — Year 4 — Year 5

Okay, so now you know how to run an effective Technology Roadmap process, but which market segments should you be selecting to do a Technology Roadmap event on? If your business serves multiple markets, should you do them all? That will be a lot of work and a huge commitment of people's time. Again, look to your business strategy for guidance. What are the key markets you intend to focus on for growth? Which are the main market segments that are growing faster than the average? Select the most important 3 or 4 market segments first and try working through the Roadmap process on those. Once you have worked through these, spend some time taking stock of the process, how it went, what you learnt, how well it is being followed up and implemented, then move on to your next program of 3 or 4 Roadmap events. Over time you will build up a business wide Technology Roadmap program, which will become part of your standard annual business event planning.

So now, having worked through some of the key aspects of 'the art of idea selection', the process of generating, assessing, filtering and processing ideas, and how they progress into the rest of the TTIP process looks like this;

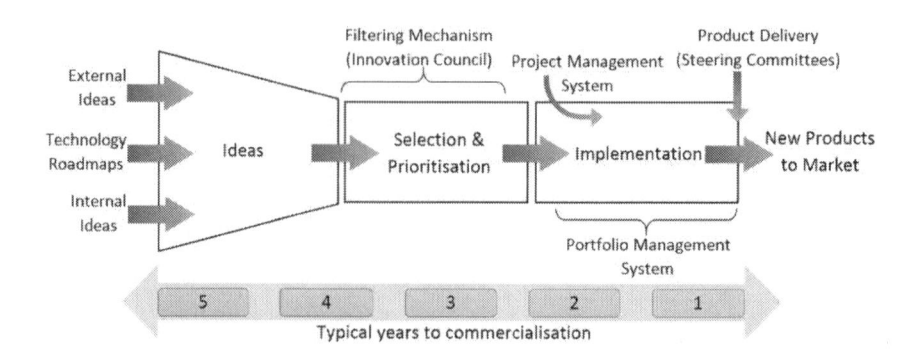

This illustrates how all the tools and techniques discussed in this book interface with each other, why each one is needed and how they all support each other. It also serves to show how the process of TTIP has to be a continuous one, with different ideas, potential projects and implementation projects all at different timescales along the continuum, with new technologies and products coming down the pipeline continually. It is important to appreciate that refreshing your ideas and product portfolio needs to be a continuous activity, there will always be a need for a blend of long term, medium term and short term opportunities.

CHAPTER 4

HOW TO MAKE YOUR IDEAS REAL – THE ART OF PROJECT MANAGEMENT

So now you have gone through the hard slog of gathering lots of ideas and potential new product and business development projects for your business. Maybe you have run a few Technology Roadmap sessions to generate ideas linked to market trends to add to your list. Your Innovation Council has assessed and prioritised them all through their chosen assessment criteria and they have finally decided which projects are worth running with. So what is the next step? How do you make your ideas real? Time to start some projects.

Project Management can be a vast subject if you want it to be. There are college courses taught on this subject all over the world, there are professional qualifications you can achieve, there are many software solutions on offer to help you with project planning. All very valuable, all very useful.

But the high level of project management rigour that they teach is only truly vital for the biggest and most complex investment projects, when you are spending multi-million and multi-billion dollar budgets on infrastructure, EPC and construction projects. The vast majority of TTIP projects you will be managing in your business will not be on this scale.

First Principles

When you first learn in your career about project management tools and techniques, you naturally start to apply everything you have learnt to all your projects. But you can soon discover that you are spending more time filling in forms than managing the team and doing the project. What I have learnt about applying project management tools, is that it is all about getting the balance right and appropriate for the scale of the project and for the level of risk involved. If project management form filling is eating up your time, this may point to a resource issue, and maybe you need to consider hiring someone to fill out the forms? Alternatively, you may be using too many and too complex tools for the scale of your project. To answer this, you need to understand the value and risk involved in the project.

If you are spending 10 billion dollars on building a new semiconductor factory for making memory chips in China over a 2 year timescale, you need to have every avenue explored and accounted for; the stakes are high. You need to have a fully qualified, world class project management professional, who will bring all the right tools to bear on the task. That factory is there to make your company 100s of billions of dollars over the next 10-15 years. But if you have a 100,000 dollar budget to cover lab and scale up work on a potential new materials technology to develop a consumable for the aluminium industry that might make a few million dollars sales, you do not need the same level of project management rigour. It is all about pitching things right. The bigger the value at stake, the more effort needs to go into project management.

To accommodate this reality, I have developed three levels of project management tool sets that I use, each adding more complexity and control as the value and risk in a project increases;

1) For the most simple, lower value projects, the only thing I insist on is an overall Gantt chart, with the project name, objectives and deliverables listed at the top. Typically such projects might have less than 1 year timeline, and budgets below 50,000 dollars. Sometimes there may not even be an assigned budget for such smaller projects, and so trying to manage a project budget in such cases is a pointless exercise. Typical projects in this category are simple redesigns or reformulations of existing products.

2) For more complex, higher value projects, I insist on running the Gantt chart, plus I add a 'Project Tracker' document, which is a single spreadsheet based document, which adds an additional layer of complexity below the Gantt chart, breaking down tasks, deliverables, milestones and adding a simple element of budgeting. This extra layer of detail helps manage team meetings and project progress effectively, without the significant burden of form filling that a full Phase Gate system requires. Typically such projects might have a 1 to 2 year timeline, and budgets below 250,000 dollars.

3) For the most complex, big value projects, I still insist

on running the Gantt chart, but then I use the full 'Phase Gate' project management documentation (we will dig into this later in the Chapter). This employs a full suite of project management tools on the project – risk analysis, budgeting, financial tools, Phase Gate checklists, IP controls, etc. Typically such projects might have a 2+ year timeline, and budgets above 250,000 dollars.

What threshold levels you set to trigger the use of each project management tool set depends completely on the size of your business and the degree of risk you are prepared to tolerate. Development projects are a gamble. You are investing in your future. It is not that different to placing a bet on the roulette table, or investing in stock, or setting up your own business. The only difference is the level of control you have over the outcome. But no matter how much control you have over the bet you are placing, there will always be forces at work which are outside your control. Everyone involved in TTIP needs to understand this when they are reviewing potential sales, and the new business pipeline, from all your new product and new business development activities. Projects can fail, projects get killed, usually for the right reason, but sometimes for the wrong reason (but only time really answers that). This book is all about helping you minimise the risk of project failure and maximise the chance of your bet paying out.

You will notice in the list above, that in every case, I always insist on every project having a simple 1 page overall Gantt chart. As I have said before, I am a great fan of one page summaries, and for project management, there is no better one page summary than a simple chart displaying key project activities and milestones versus time. As projects get more complex, and teams get bigger, it is very easy for people to get lost in the detail of the project and lose sight of what the whole project is actually trying to achieve. Too often in project team meetings, discussions can get stuck on some minute detail, because individuals can get very passionate about the things they are working on. Whilst you want to fuel the passion, and it is all very creditable, as a project manager and chair of the meeting, you need to constantly remind people of the bigger picture of the overall task and bring people back to plan. You will need to constantly reinforce this message, so that the team does not forget where you're all heading, and there is no better method than maintaining a Gantt chart, with the objectives and deliverables listed at the top. This gives perspective and helps the team make decisions about what is important and what is not important so that everyone is clear about where the project is and what the goals are.

In preparing a Gantt chart, there is certainly an art to choosing what the key activities are. Junior project managers can also get wrapped up in the detail of their projects, and in their enthusiasm they can be tempted to write down far too many detailed tasks in the Gantt chart. This is usually in an effort to show how busy they are. It is an important skill to develop to be able to group and summarise actions and one that is very important to learn in terms of effective communication. I always emphasize this to all staff that I have managed and individuals I have mentored, and subsequently spend much time coaching them in this technique. It does not come naturally to everyone. Insisting on a one page version, such that the chart will fit comfortably on a screen or as a single slide in a presentation, forces the project manager to think really hard about grouping and summarising activities, because there is rarely enough space on a slide to list more than 10 key activities. The times I have sat through project presentations, where the presenter puts up their project Gantt chart on the screen and it is just completely illegible because it has dozens (or more) of rows of activities on there. Again, I believe it is simply an effort to show they are doing lots of work, but as an audience member, I can tell you, at best it communicates nothing, at worst it shows that the person is not an effective communicator. So not a good idea and not recommended. Learn to summarise.

Your Gantt chart is not only a great project management tool, it is also a very important communication tool, ideal for when you are presenting progress not only to the team, but also to senior management. Having a visual means to display project progress and direction is always much more easy to digest for an audience than having a text based list of activities versus dates, which I have seen used many times in presentations. If you're looking to keep senior management on your side, to be enthused by what you're doing, to support the investment and resourcing decisions that you will need in your project, and presuming you're looking for promotion, then the ability to summarise and communicate in a simple, clear, easily understood way is vital.

There are many software packages and free spreadsheet templates available to help you prepare a Gantt chart, but honestly, I just prepare it from scratch every time, maintaining a standard look and feel each time. It is very simple to do, but the reason I do it this way is that since you are building from scratch, it forces you to think really deeply about your project tasks and time line.

Building a Proposal and Project Budgeting

One of the key deciders in what level of project management tools you choose to use for a project is budget. Project budgeting and tracking spend are obviously very important in terms of managing your investment. But depending on the scale of the business and the size of the project, what I have observed, having worked with many businesses, is that not every company has the financial processes set up to track spend by project. This is usually because their cost control is based on traditional departmental and functional splits, and in some cases, with smaller projects, no specific budget may even be assigned and the costs just get rolled up into an overall R&D budget. In such cases, setting up the capability to track project budgets within an organisation is not a simple or straightforward task, and is usually a project in itself. Decisions have to be made about which cost centres to pull data from and then mechanisms put in place to reliably collect, collate and report the numbers. A fundamental issue is what aspects of spend do you include in a project budget? There are plenty of direct project costs, such as consumables, travel, full time project staff, etc. which are clear cut. But what about all the indirect costs? What about the time invested by the project team members who are only part time? Some may be technical staff working on more than one project, some will be sales people, some operational and process engineering staff. The time invested by these people will change as the project evolves. Sales and business development staff will invest more time in the project as customer trials need arranging and managing, and as the project launch date gets closer, with marketing staff joining in. Marketing budget will need to be spent to create product literature and to fund a launch event. Process engineering and operational staff will become more involved during production trials and building quality control plans. And what about you as the project manager? Should your costs be included? Are you dedicated to this one project? Or do you have other projects and other duties to perform? How should you budget for all this? This can start to get complex.

It is frequently the case that only direct project costs get assigned to a project budget. The costs of non-core team members are usually considered sunk costs as they are fully budgeted in their respective departments. Marketing literature also usually has its own budget, so such costs don't get assigned to a project. Whilst this makes life easier in terms of capturing financial data and monitoring spend, it can be somewhat misleading because it does not give a real sense of scale of how much the business is really investing in a project. Production trials can frequently become a source of debate if they became expensive and they are not budgeted anywhere, because up to a point they are absorbed into production costs, but when trials start to affect production schedules and meeting KPIs, the production team tend to start to squeal.

So setting a project budget is not as clear cut as it may first seem. By including only direct project costs, you may end up with a comparatively small number and only have visibility of just the R&D or processing engineering parts of the project; the hard costs. By not tracking the soft costs (indirect, sunk costs, marketing costs, etc.) it really gives a false impression of just how much the company is investing in the project. With the traditional accounting approach, the reality is such that as the project manager, you might just be looking at the R&D bit of your project, with a 100,000 dollar price tag. But when you start to add in the 500,000 dollars that the production scale up and all the customer trial runs are going to cost, and the 300,000 dollars for the costs of all the part-time multi-functional team members, and the 100,000 dollars for marketing literature and launch event (i.e. when you consider the 'total' resources that a business is actually throwing at a project to take it from initial idea to profitable sales), your little 100,000 dollar R&D project can actually be costing the business a million dollars. The difference between the quoted project budget and the true costs of the project to a business can easily be ten times or more.

Let us be clear, the traditional accounting approach which gives us the lower figure is done because it is easy. It is a result of the inward looking internal structure of our businesses. It is one of the consequences of 'too much internal focus' (see Chapter 2), the same internal focus that gives rise to separately managed functions and organisational silos. It is taking the easy route from the ground up, instead of taking a top down view, which is the view that a business really should be taking when making investment decisions, which is exactly what a new product or new business development project is, an investment decision. You can grow your business be investing in more production capacity, by investing in acquiring a new business to add technology or market share to your portfolio, or by investing in developing new technology and products internally. If you want to make balanced, informed decisions on your investment portfolio, you really need to be judging the cost, risk, and reward elements in the same way across your investment options. If you were planning on acquiring a new business, you would not expect the acquisition costs to be out by ten times would you? If you were planning a capital investment on a new factory, you would not expect costs to overrun by ten times would you? 5-10% maybe, but not ten times. So why do businesses regularly under report their costs of new business and new product development by up to ten times?

Senior Management and Company boards are regularly fooling themselves that they have the right facts in front of them for investment decisions. I know, I have been there on many occasions. I have been as guilty as anyone in my early Board career of looking at such numbers and not appreciating what they really represent and not considering that they do not represent like with like. This is clearly dangerous ground when it comes to project prioritisation, project kill/cure decisions and investment decisions. So wherever you choose to draw the line in project budgeting, you need to establish some company-wide rules about what you will and will not include in project budgets.

So, we have seen that the true costs of a new technology, new product or new business development project are not easily determined, and more than that, they can and will be fluid, as they will change through the life of a project. As a project progresses and tracks through each phase gate, this gives better visibility of the likely costs involved. Right at the start of a project, as you are assessing the initial idea (see Chapter 3) and preparing the Project Definition document, your budget is always going to just be a best guess. You may break it down into lots of detail to add some logic and justification to your budget estimate, but it is just that, an estimate. As the project progresses, things will happen that you did not, or could not, anticipate, changing project direction, resource needs, timescales and inevitably, the budget. Sure, you need cost control, you need detail, you need relevance and reality, but given the ambiguity inherent in budgeting, at least at the front end of the project, obviously a balance has to be drawn up between trying to track absolutely every minute detail that contributes to a project (which could become another gross non-value added time waster), and having some mechanism that at least appreciates the bigger chunks of cost that are or will be contributing fully to a project.

Which brings us to another classic dilemma of project

budgeting. Why do so many projects over run and over spend? You hear often in the media, of big government infrastructure projects being delayed by months or sometimes years, and overspending by x billions of dollars. Why is this? This same thing happens regularly in industry, I am sure you have seen plenty of such projects in your business, maybe you were the project manager on one? One reason is certainly the unexpected, unanticipated things that happen as a project progresses, a really big curve ball can have a significant impact, sometimes even killing a project. Another is simply bad management. But one frequently common factor is linked to budgeting, the way projects are under-budgeted and oversold at the start. Right at the start of the investment decision, someone has to stand before senior management and present the project to get a go/no-go decision on funding. So what do they do? They sell the benefits as best they can and then it comes to the bottom line, how much will it cost? What are the typical responses you get? It's too expensive? Can you do it for less? Can you deliver it faster? These are all fair and reasonable challenges, but what happens next time the same person presents a new project pitch? They have already gauged what is acceptable on cost and timescale, so they start to chip away at the budget and the timescale before they present. But then they get the same responses and so the cycle continues. Before you know it, you are presenting a project budget that is cut to the bone and over committing delivery because you know that's how you get it past senior management. Then try as hard as you may, 2 years later, you find your project over budget and late delivering. It is a perpetual cycle that I have seen many times. This creates a culture of overselling projects because that's how people know they can get it funded. The result is an organisation that routinely overcommits and underperforms on its new business development and capital expenditure projects. This is another classic scenario in business where you need to inject a dose of reality into proceedings.

At some point in the process of budgeting and project pitching, the budget was probably at the stage of best estimate. Presuming there was a little extra built in for a rainy day at the start, which then gets cut back, and then gets cut out. The capital cost may have been a bit generous, then cut to realistic, then cut more and becomes challenging to really achieve. The project team costs may have had an extra person for comfort at the start, but then gets whittled down to a skeleton crew by the end. At some point it was the best, most realistic estimate it could be, given the many uncertainties in the project at that stage. At this point in the process, the whole team needs to take stock and be honest, and above all be realistic about what this project, this investment is likely to cost up front.

There are a couple of practical tips to project budgeting I have learnt along the way and from having seen too many projects over spend, too many times;

1) Add a 10 or 20% risk factor onto the budget – Whatever the final budget is, add 10 or 20% on top of this, depending on the level of risk involved. If the project is something you have done before, like building a second, identical production line, then the level of risk is going to be relatively low. But generally, your investment decisions will be on new facilities, new product development, and new business development activities, which because they are 'new' have a higher level of risk involved, so don't be afraid to add 20% to the final costs. Believe me, you will need it. It doesn't matter how much

planning you do up front, how many risk scenarios you consider, there will always be something that comes along during the project that you hadn't considered, in some cases, some things which could never be anticipated. The bigger and more complex the project, the more likely that a curve ball will arrive at some point. So add 20% to the budget.

2) If your project is to build a factory, or a new production line, then make sure you fund the design phase before you finalise the budget. The times I have seen capex submitted for new factories, based on a best guess at building costs at the start. Everyone always tries to break it down into lots of detail and tries to consider as much as possible, but people rarely get it all in there. Back to the previous point, there will always be things you didn't consider, such as local planning fees from some government department you weren't aware of. Building a factory is complicated, you won't think of everything. The difference here is that you actually have a chance of getting the budget right. If you consider the project pitch as Phase 1, and just get the funding agreed to design and cost the factory, then you can arrive at the exact cost without overcommitting on the total project budget. Treat this as funding a feasibility phase. It may still cost a lot to pay a company to design and cost and make an offer, but then you can go into the next round of funding with your eyes open and make the appropriate decision to move forward with the actual build or not. It is much better this way than commit to the whole project on a shoestring factory build budget, then find out you run out of money part of the way through the build, because that is almost inevitable. Funding a feasibility

design stage gives you realistic costs so that you can make the right investment decision for your business.

The Phase Gate Project Management System

The classic, and now routine, approach to managing a new technology and new product development project through the innovation funnel, is the Phase Gate project management system (see Chapter 1). Following acceptance of a Project Proposal (which is usually referred to as Phase 0), the project is typically split into 5 'Phases', which is where the project work progresses, and is managed on a daily basis though Gantt charts, action planning, scheduling, etc. Each Phase has a 'Gate' which is a critical decision point, usually in the form of a full team meeting, and based around a system of structured, methodical checklists, at which Go/Kill/Hold/Cure decisions are made on the project. Having a companywide standardised Phase Gate approach to project management has a number of advantages. It's disciplined, structured framework provides a regular heartbeat to the project. It forces ownership, accountability and decisions to be made. Its multi-functional team approach promotes collaboration and cross-functional team working, and if managed correctly, it will 'Transform Technology into Profit' for the business.

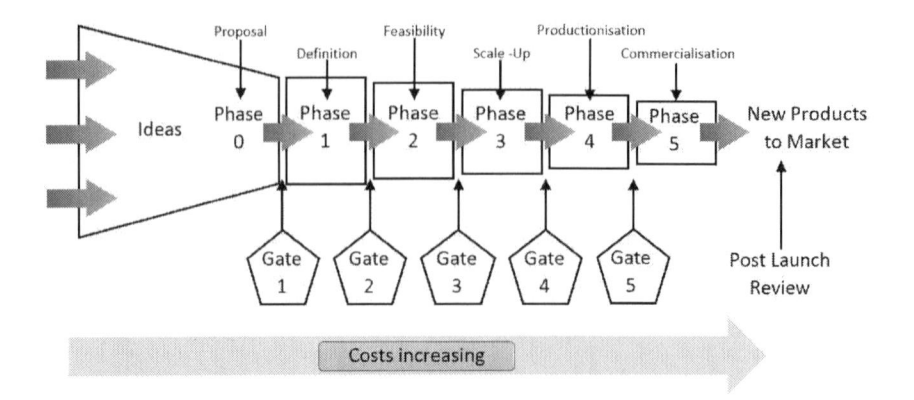

Like many of the classic project management and innovation tools mentioned in this book, there is much published on the Phase Gate Project Management system and its variations, and lots of companies offering spreadsheet templates to assist with managing the Phases and Gates, so I do not intend to regurgitate an exhaustive guide to Phase Gate systems in this book. But I will give you my thoughts on key things to look out for in each of the Phases and Gates, what the most useful aspects of such project documentation are and how best to use them. All the separate Phase and Gate documents should each run no more than one page, and they should all fit comfortably together in one spreadsheet document, each as a separate tab. This keeps all project documentation together in one place, and allows for easy central filing and recording of Gate signatories, and for managing version updates for the whole team.

Phase 0) Project Proposal – a project proposal document is a much more challenging thing to produce than most people realise. Many times I have had people come to me with good ideas, particularly sales people out on the road.

Their real expectation is that they tell me their idea and I then get someone to work on it, but of course that's not going to happen without plenty of upfront validation, so I always ask them to fill in a very simple, one page project proposal document, asking very simple, clear questions about what it is, what it will do, what is the advantage, what is the target market, target application, target customers, any competitors, etc., addressing all the assessment criteria (Strategic, Technical & Resource) used in the 'Ideas List' (see Chapter 3). 70% of the time I never hear from the person again. I train all my senior team in this technique now. Of the other 30%, they make some attempt at completing the document, but usually need a lot of help, because they have not thought through what they are asking (which is the point of having the document of course). 90% of the draft proposals I get back have a complete lack of market data. The person with the idea has no clue as to the potential market size or potential sales, just that it feels like a good idea. So in order to truly assess an idea, the idea first needs support to flesh it out, and usually this means getting a technical or applications person to help with building on the idea and a marketing person involved to help with market data. Another key source of project proposals is from the Technology Roadmap sessions (see Chapter 3). All potential projects identified by the Roadmapping process should have an owner assigned to them who should prepare a project proposal document.

Gate 1) Project Proposal Sign Off – all the project proposal documents from all sources in Phase 0, go onto the 'Ideas List' and through the Innovation Council for assessment. If they get approved as a project, then they will move onto Phase 1 for preparation of a full Project Definition. Gate 1 needs to be a portfolio decision of whether this project is worthy to work on in comparison to all the other potential projects, not a team decision about whether it is a good project or not. Therefore I have learnt to take this first go/no-go decision to the Innovation Council for a bigger picture view. Gate 1 is essentially about signing off the project proposal. Signatories should be the senior members of the Innovation Council. As long at the proposal is completed using a standardised template, it will be very easy to see if there is any important information missing, and beyond that it is down to the quality of the proposal. You basically have to answer the question; given all the other proposals on the table, does this project offer a compelling enough business case?

Phase 1) Project Definition – it is absolutely vital to have a very clear, well documented, well researched and validated definition of what the project is trying to achieve, agreed by all the players, before the team starts work on the project. It will save the business a lot of wasted time and money later on. You absolutely must have this before you launch into doing the project. The Definition document must cover the scope of the project, the objectives, a time and resource plan (both an overall Gantt chart and a detailed planning document), an IP scorecard, a financial scorecard and a basic risk analysis. This is also the stage where you will be setting the Project Targets (sometimes called an ID Card), which includes a broad range of product performance ('what it does'), product characteristics ('what it is'), production costs, margin and other commercial targets, and safe use targets (e.g. certifications required). These need a lot of thought and debate, and define what the project needs to achieve to be deemed complete and a success. Whatever numbers you decide on need to be clear and unambiguous and SMART (Specific, Measurable,

Achievable, Relevant, Time-bound). This is a key challenge for the project, because the more targets you set and the tougher they are to achieve, the longer and more costly will be the project, reducing the chance of success. Equally, if you set the targets too soft, you may end up with a new product that doesn't quite do what the customer needs it to do or doesn't differentiate itself sufficiently from competitive offerings, and you run the risk of falling short of delivering what the project set out to achieve in the first place. To find a happy medium, since any technical project ends up with a long list of targets, a useful technique is to rank all the targets in terms of 2 categories, 'essential' and 'nice to have', using a colour coding system on your spreadsheet for clarity. This way, you keep all the targets in view, but if you fall short of a couple of 'nice to haves' then it doesn't kill the project and you can still deliver a profitable outcome. The Project Definition document, along with the associated Project Planning and Project Targets documents, will live with you throughout the entire life of the project. You will need to constantly refer to them to keep things on track, to remain in scope and to refine your plan as the project progresses. You may also need to modify the Project Targets as the project progresses, as you learn more about the target application and get feedback from customer trials. The project definition phase is not just about sitting in a meeting room planning the project and agreeing targets. It will also very likely require some degree of practical early concept development work in the laboratory and certainly will involve visiting customers to understand the application first hand. This is usually necessary to be able to set targets with confidence. So in Phase 1, you will likely be exploring the technology platform underpinning the new product, such that during Phase 2 you will build on this to refine the platform into a more practical and exploitable form.

Gate 2) Project Definition Sign Off – this is the meeting at which the team decides if the Project Definition document meets all the checklist criteria to release for starting the feasibility work. This, and all subsequent, Gate meetings should involve the whole project team, and because they are structured around the Gate checklist, they should be a relatively quick session, no more than 30 minutes. Gate meetings should not become big debates, the required deliverables should be unambiguous in the checklist and the data presented should make it clear whether these have been delivered or not. If the meeting takes longer than 30 minutes, then this indicates that you are not really ready for the Gate decision. Gate decisions will normally be (near) unanimous, because any 'debates' should have already happened during project team meetings during the Phase work. It is good practice to schedule the next Gate meeting at the end of each Gate. This is likely to be several months into the future, but this provides an important milestone for the project team to work towards. Formal sign off is done by the senior team members (often called the Gatekeepers), who will be the business leads for technology, sales, operations, etc. and all be members of the Innovation Council.

Phase 2) Feasibility – this is where the bulk of the R&D work gets done in a project, working through proof of concept and leading to prototyping, either still at the lab scale or on a pilot line. The working prototype needs to meet all the 'essential' target performance criteria, preferably including field testing results. Project planning details will have gained more depth by this stage, with more detailed timescale and financial plans for the rest of the

Phases developed. The Intellectual Property landscape should also be well understood by now, with invention disclosure forms completed, patent searches and clarity on 'freedom to operate'. You may already be choosing to file patent applications if the new technology warrants it. If the project is developing a new Technology Platform, then it will likely stay in Phase 2 for a long time, sometimes up to 2 years, until the commercial direction becomes more targeted, new product designs are established, and it can move into Phase 3. This is where the Phase Gate process can become a struggle to use for basic R&D departments and it can become quite demoralising to a team sitting in Phase 2 for 2 years. I have seen such teams split Phase 2 into 4 sub-phases to try to generate some level of structure and to provide a sense of progress to the team.

Gate 3) Prototype Sign Off – this is the meeting at which the team decides if the prototype meets the Project Targets for release for scale up production runs.

Phase 3) Scale Up – this is where the first small scale production runs of the prototypes are made. There may be a move from a pilot line to a full production line for the first time and the production runs may still be small volume at this stage but growing larger with each production trial. Raw material sourcing routes will start to be explored and early supply negotiations will begin. Scale up is where many practical issues will appear in terms of how to control production with respect to material specifications, impurity levels, dimensional tolerances, pressure and temperature settings, etc. Some of these will have limitations based around your manufacturing process and some of these will be minimum requirements needed in the target application(s). Therefore, it is important to keep in regular customer contact throughout this phase in order to make sure that the boundaries set by the process do not force you down a track that would make the product unfit for use at the customer. So field trials will increase in frequency and the range of customers involved. Scale up is often the most challenging phase of the whole project. Developing the technology and creating a working prototype can happen reasonably quickly, certainly in a matter of months, after which there can be a touch of euphoria in the team that you have cracked the problem, and that the hard work is over. Certainly at this point the technology is essentially considered developed and the team and the sponsors generally breathe a sigh of relief, and there is a general expectation that the project is almost complete. In my experience, this can lead to a period of significant frustration for some project sponsors who feel that the technology or product is developed so what's the hold up, let's just get on and launch it. The harsh reality is that if the Definition and Feasibility phases take 6 months, then it is not untypical for Scale Up and Productionisation to take 12 to 24 months. This is because in reality, moving into scale up always brings up many more problems than you could have imagined and can be a real hard slog for the team. You inevitably discover things you did not know about the technology you have developed, all of which need working through because in the end you need a robust technology that can be manufactured at scale, reproducibly and within acceptable tolerances to meet quality requirements, otherwise you will have no saleable product. Therefore significant process engineering input is usually required during Phase 3, and you will be throwing consumables and teams of people at the problems, so costs ramp up, particularly as you will likely be producing rejects as you first scale up production trials. The outline production process route will be emerging and a full FMEA (Failure Mode Effect Analysis) on the product design will be needed.

Gate 4) Pre-production Sign Off – this is the meeting at which the team decides if the new product is ready for release for larger production runs.

Phase 4) Productionisation – this is where the production prototype becomes a product that can be manufactured at scale, repeatably and reliably. This phase will involve preparing Standard Operating Procedures, training shop floor workers, building a quality control plan and a full FMEA on the manufacturing process. These will lock down all those production criteria investigated during Phase 3 and form the overall production manual for the new product. This will trigger product specification sign off by customers for the first time, acknowledging that there will be no more product tweaking. Raw material supply negotiations will be finalised and sourcing routes fully established. Commercially, you will be launching larger scale customer trials and probably testing the product in a wider set of environments, based around the core application, to determine the product's working boundaries. Production costing & product pricing will also be refined during Phase 4. Any patent applications you chose to file early in the project should be at a fairly mature stage by now. A particular challenge in Phases 3 and 4 is getting time scheduled on production lines. Unless the need is well understood by the production team and scheduled in as early as possible, the business will always put standard production runs first. This can be a frustrating time for the project team, as without careful planning, there can be long periods of low activity between production runs. There is also some tendency of production management not wanting to put prototype products onto their production lines because they are not yet 'ready for production' and will make their KPIs look bad, e.g. increase rejects. This is very 'chicken and egg', because unless the new product gets time on production to iron out the wrinkles it will never get production ready. This is where having pilot scale facilities can be a real bonus for the project team. You also need to sort out up front how the business is going to account for production runs. Will the production data count towards operational KPIs? Are the products going to be sold to a customer or used for internal testing? So do not underestimate the time and resources you will need to push a project through Productionisation, I have found this to be the single most underestimated phase of the whole Phase Gate process. To speed things up you can try to throw more people and cash at the problem, but usually the single biggest influence on the rate of getting through this phase is getting time on production, so if a business really wants this new product launched, it really has to put its money where its mouth is and handover production time to the project team. This is a tough and expensive decision. Not only can Productionisation take twice as much time to complete as the previous 3 project phases, but I have also found that early in the project when the budgets are being prepared, the project leader can have a tendency to gloss over the expense that is heading your way at Productionisation, because there is a belief that if the true costs of the project are made clear early on, then the project will not be given the go ahead (see Project Budgeting earlier in this Chapter). This is part of the politics of getting project approvals. The project leader hopes that if they get a successful Technology developed then the business will be swept up in the euphoria of success and fund the subsequent stages. This is a risky game, but I've seen it play out positively and negatively, so you just have to know your players. Ideally, if you educate the business that the big time and cost will come in Productionisation, there should be no surprises.

Gate 5) Production Sign Off – this is the meeting at which the team decides if the new product meets all the criteria for full production and is ready for official release to the market.

Phase 5) Commercialisation – your new product may already have had some early sales through large scale customer trials in earlier phases, but Phase 5 is when everything is ready for the official launch. Product specifications will now be fixed, no more changes allowed. The production locations will have been agreed. Marketing literature will be prepared, the sales campaign and business plan will be established and a launch event organised (see Chapter 7). Once this phase is finished, the project is effectively considered complete. The product launch process can be fraught with frustrations, as there is always pressure to launch before all the reproducibility and repeatability issues in production are under full quality control. This is the value of the Phase Gate checklist and having clear targets, but some of these targets inevitably get challenged right at the end to facilitate launch ('do we really need a tolerance of dimension x?'). Obviously, launching and building sales takes time, but is influenced heavily by how passionately the business believes in the new product.

Post Launch Review) this is not strictly a gate, since the product is launched now, but it is important. This is the stage that I see missed out time and time again. Businesses often have systems requiring capex project post-implementation reviews and new product launch reviews, but because everyone is already busy working on the next project, they get ignored. The result of this is there is no real clarity of whether a project truly was a success or not, no appreciation of what worked and didn't in the process and the same failures of process occur again and again. My advice is, at the end of the Gate 5 meeting, agree the date for the Post Launch Review and put it in everyone's diaries. Typically this is 12 months away, but that's fine, at least there is a marker in the sand.

Intellectual Property Management

Whilst you are working towards TTIP, one key subject you will need to address is Intellectual Property. The Phase Gate project management process has IP woven into its system of Gate documents, so forces you to address this early on and throughout the life of a project. Like other functional areas in any project, IP requires specialist skills, so ideally you should have access to an IP lawyer as part of your team or alternatively on a 3rd party consultancy basis. Too often I have worked in businesses where the technical lead and the technical team are expected to cover this function and this presents some challenges.

It is vitally important right at the outset to understand that IP is fundamentally a commercial tool. There is often a misconception in business that the technology department handles the IP, and this is because they are usually the ones that spend the most time on writing the patent, if that is the route the project team decides to go down, but in fact the main reasons to publish patents are to protect your sales or block competitive activity in a market. This whole misconception usually means that the commercial team keeps as far away from IP as possible. With every senior technology job I ever did, one of my responsibilities was always IP portfolio management, which primarily means patents and trademarks. This always seemed crazy to me, and a situation that I could never resolve, as I could never find a commercial owner who wanted to take it on. The danger of all this is that IP can become a technology driven exercise, which misses the whole point of what IP is for. Just like with the whole process of TTIP, working through the parallel work stream of IP should be a collaborative exercise. Completing invention disclosure forms and preparing patents should be a combined effort by the commercial, technical and legal (i.e. the IP lawyer) functions.

When considering IP in the context of TTIP, it is usual to just think of patents, and they certainly have an important part to play in the process. But IP is actually a broader set of commercial tools, encompassing patents, trademarks, trade secrets and know how. Everyone is generally familiar with what patents and trademarks are, but not so much with the other categories. A 'Trade Secret' is information that a business deems vital and wants to restrict the knowledge and use of. Practically this means it gets written down, kept securely and has a designated owner who controls access. 'Know How' is knowledge within the business that is not typically written down or controlled in this way, but is part of the general background knowledge used to manufacture or use the business's products. A trade secret is fundamentally different from a patent, in that a patent is information written down and disclosed to the public (with legal controls), whereas a trade secret is not disclosed publically but kept controlled internally by the business. As your project progresses through the Phase Gates, the team will need to make a fundamental decision on which of these IP routes to head down to protect the new technology it is developing. To help make these decisions, the team needs a background understanding of its IP options and decision tools to help make the choice.

Another basic premise of going down the IP route to protect your company's technology, is that you should only go down the chosen route if you are prepared to actively manage the IP going forward. This is not a one-time deal. Internal IP (trade secrets and know how) is easier to handle, as an internal owner can be assigned and it is relatively easy and cheap to keep on top of things. But external IP (patents & trademarks) is much more challenging and many times more expensive because you need to pay an external legal agent to file and register documents. You will still need an internal role assigned to manage all external IP, but ultimately, external IP is only really useful as a commercial tool if you are prepared to police it, and that can mean taking people and competitors to court. This is where the costs can ramp up. Some modern tech-savvy companies have whole departments all over this on a day to day basis, and in some cases making plenty of money from cleverly managing the whole angle of lawsuits and countersuits. This is particularly prominent in the consumer electronics market, where companies can win or lose millions (and billions) of dollars on IP court decisions. However, for the majority of industrial businesses, they tend to go down the patent and trademark route because they feel they need to do something to provide protection for their hard earned secrets, but then do a poor job of policing their patents and trademarks.

We have established that IP is a commercial tool. It is there to sustain the profits generated by your new product and new business development activities for as long as possible, to maximise the return from your development investments. It does this by putting legal barriers in place to prevent a 3rd party copying your technology and/or brands. This can have a variety of commercial benefits, e.g. generating sales, strengthening reputation, blocking market access, adding strength to contract negotiations and gaining the 'freedom to operate' in a market. If you have done your TTIP right, then you can expect high profits from being the first to market, but these will quickly disappear if you do not work to protect your position. IP gives you one means to achieve this.

There are 3 fundamental approaches with IP;

1) Defensive – to defend a current position as a market and technology leader and maintain your existing profit stream.
2) Aggressive – to control market positioning by blocking competitive access to grow your profit margin.
3) Growth – to help gain access to targeted new markets to deliver sales growth.

For guidance on which approach is appropriate and the balance you should maintain between the three, you should refer to your business strategy. To apply each approach successfully you need to have a very good understanding of the markets you are playing in or have targeted for growth. That includes key suppliers, customer base, main competitors, and threats from potential new entrants and technology substitution. As a project develops and the technology and product development matures, so does our knowledge of the addressed market. Therefore the approach you choose to take may change over time. Control of the information generated during a project therefore becomes vitally important in managing the future IP situation for the business, and appropriate steps should be put in place. This is why non-disclosure agreements (NDAs) have become the norm everywhere you turn in business now, written into employment contracts, and as standalone documents signed by suppliers, trial customers and other project collaborators. Public disclosure through conference presentations and published articles can form a valuable means to publicise new products and technology, but what is written should be carefully vetted against the IP strategy of the project before publication.

If a decision is made to go down the patent route, then there are a number of rules and good practices that are helpful to understand when writing the patent document. A general rule of thumb is that products and technologies that are easy to reverse engineer are best protected by patenting, whereas those that are very difficult to reverse engineer should be protected internally as trade secrets or know how. The most common type of patent you will encounter in the industrial world of TTIP is called a Utility Patent. This type of patent covers new compositions (chemistry or formulations), equipment (or devices), manufacturing processes and manufactured items. It can also cover a specific application of one of these categories. Another type of patent you may come across is called a Design Patent, which serves to protect the shape, configuration and the surface ornamentation of an object. But this is less common in industry because it only protects the object's appearance, not its function. For this you need a Utility Patent.

With respect to the increasing complexity model for new technologies and products introduced in Chapter 1, we would expect to utilise Utility Patents in each case;

1) Technology Platforms – patents have the potential to provide broad protection to multiple products, usually based on composition and/or form
2) Products – patents have the potential to provide protection to a single product group, usually based on form and/or functionality
3) Solutions – patents have the potential to provide protection to a product design group, usually based on form, functionality and/or structure
4) Systems – patents have the potential to provide protection to a product design group, usually based on functionality and/or structure

To decide which route to go with patenting, in terms of focusing on composition, form, functionality, structure or application, and whether your commercial driver is defensive, aggressive or growth, your business needs to develop an IP strategy which supports your overall business strategy. You also need to decide some minimum criteria for patenting, after all, not every new product is worth the expense of patenting. These rules normally have a minimum market value threshold, coupled with a checklist to verify that prior art searches and an invention disclosure form have been completed. And you also need to decide the market coverage you are aiming for with your protection. Is it one country, one region, global? At some point you will need to select countries and regions, because this targets IP protection. This can become a tricky decision, particularly if you are filing early in your project, and one where you need access to current business sales and sales projections for your new product. This is where it really needs to be a commercially driven exercise, not one driven by the technical person writing the patent. Whether you start with national phase entry or broader PCT (Patent

Cooperation Treaty) filings, the filing process normally gives you plenty of time to shift direction and refine your country coverage as the patent application progresses. This is where a professional IP lawyer is essential in helping you manage your way through the complex international processes. Country selection is important because each country you choose to protect in will cost you money, not only the upfront fee, but also the future renewal fees for the next 20 years. Over this timescale you will inevitably find that markets change and you will be making decisions on renewals and asking yourself 'why did we patent in Argentina or in Thailand?' Some of these decisions are just lost in the mists of time, others were because in the past there was a poor appreciation of the IP process and there were often blanket decisions to just protect everywhere.

Having decided the nature and focus of the patent application you intend to prepare, there are many rules and best practice that you really need to know to prepare the most robust patent that offers the maximum protection for your technology. Preparation of a patent application should be a joint activity between technical and legal, because the structure of the document itself contains legal sections (Field, Summary, and Claims) and technical sections (Background, Description, Examples). The infamous 'patent speak' used by patent lawyers, obvious to anyone that has ever tried to read a patent, is crucial here in terms of getting the right legal phraseology to build a strong, defendable legal document. However you work through building up the document, there are some overall tactics you need to have at the front of your mind. To get your patent application through the examination process, your 'Claims' must be clear, unambiguous, novel, inventive (as established by your experimental data in your Examples) and define the invention, your 'Description' must enable someone 'skilled in the art' to reproduce your invention. To maximise the benefit of the patent to your business, your 'Claims' need to be easily detectable so that you can spot them out in the market, and should work best in combination with your internal trade secrets and know how. This latter is tricky to achieve, given the level of disclosure a patent requires to meet the examination criteria, but should be the ultimate scenario you aim for.

One common situation in a project with respect to writing a patent application is that lots of experimental work gets done in Phase 1 and certainly in Phase 2 to develop the base technology, with the aim of developing the target new product. But when all this information is brought together to start preparing the patent application, there are gaps in the information with respect to writing the claims, and more work has to be done to gather the necessary information, particularly with respect to exploring and establishing the boundaries. Sometimes this work can be considerable, diverting resources, and at times can take over from the core activity of developing the new product. This takes careful management to deliver sufficient information to prepare a robust patent application, whilst at the same time trying to progress the main stream of development activity to create the new product.

CHAPTER 5

HOW TO TAKE PEOPLE WITH YOU – THE ART OF LEADING AND MANAGING TEAMS

For innovation and new product development to be successful, of course process is important. All the templates, spreadsheets and checklists we use are important for bringing order to the chaos and for helping to make sense of the huge amounts of data you have to work through, but all of this will not bring you success on its own, will not deliver you successful new products. Why? Because innovation is primarily about people. You can bring all the process you want to the party, but if you do not have the skills and experience to lead and manage teams and to get people to work together and to buy into the new process, success will not follow.

Project Team Roles

Every project team must have clear roles and responsibilities assigned and be resourced appropriately. One of the advantages of the Phase Gate project management approach, is that it promotes multi-functional team membership and therefore encourages cross functional collaboration between both senior management and the project team member levels. The critical roles that must be assigned are;

1) Project Leader or manager (although I prefer the term Project Owner) – it is absolutely critical for the success of any project that one person has ownership. Projects will usually have more than one senior person involved, e.g. a sales lead and a technical lead, but there must only be one project owner, otherwise things will start to fall between the cracks. There must be only one person who has overall responsibility, who wakes up in the morning thinking about how to progress the project, and who reports on the project to management. This person is responsible for maintaining the discipline of the entire Phase Gate process. They will be organising and chairing all the meetings and managing project data and documentation. Some tasks they may delegate to other team members, but they cannot delegate the responsibility of ownership, that must always sit with the project leader.
2) Project Sponsor – this must be a senior person, preferably a member of the Board or Executive and the Innovation Council. Like the project leader role, the sponsor must be a single individual. The role of the sponsor is to support the project leader

throughout the whole organisation, unblocking functional barriers, co-opting new skills into the team when required, and championing the project at the senior management level. They should act as coach and mentor to the project leader, and they should hold accountability for delivery of the project at the highest level. The sponsor should feel he has 'skin in the game' and should be supporting and encouraging the project leader to deliver the project goals on time and on budget. The project sponsor will normally also be one of the official sign off gatekeepers and act as chairperson for this group.

3) Team Members – the project leader must assemble a team with the appropriate range of skills needed to make the project happen, including technology, operations, sales, engineering, finance, IP, etc. The project sponsor will likely need to assist with bringing some of these individuals into the team through negotiation with their bosses. There is a tendency on big projects to assemble big teams, but this can create a lot of dysfunction. It is best to keep any team below 10 people (including the project leader and other team roles). The team members will in some cases have subordinates or teams below them to do the actual work, but it is usually not appropriate to bring all of these people into a team meeting, and the team member should act to represent all of their group's activities in the project. Individuals can come and go as part of the project team, as the project progresses and a different blend of skills become needed in the different phases, but there should always remain a core of team membership to provide continuity and momentum.

4) Gatekeepers – these are the senior management

members that provide the official sign off at the Gate meetings. These are the individuals that need to be convinced that real progress is being made. They usually make up about one third of the project team and include the Project Sponsor. They should remain throughout the whole of the project to provide stability and will likely be acting in this role on several project teams. Gatekeepers are effectively the project Steering Committee, and should work to ensure that the project maintains relevance and sticks to its scope. They can be very useful in bringing other resources into the team as needed and in providing a wealth of contacts for the project team to tap into.

Managing a large team of people always presents its own unique challenges because you are not just trying to manage a team of functional skills and expertise, you are also trying to manage a bunch of people and personalities, which is where the fun begins. Check back to Chapter 2 for some of the behaviours you are likely to meet along the way which will challenge you, the progress of your project and the Phase Gate process itself.

There are many good tools and techniques available for understanding the dynamics within your team and what drives the individual behaviours you will have to deal with (including your own). The Belbin Team Inventory analyses personality types and their behavioural preferences against a set of defined team roles. This can help with clarifying the strengths and weaknesses of team members. The Myers-Briggs Type Indicator assesses an individual's personality. This can help with improving self-awareness in team members in understanding how and why they behave the way they do. Team mapping techniques analyse the quality and intensity of interactions between individuals in a team to identify the weak links and where relationships need to be improved. These are three of the classic, standard tools, but there are many others available. There are software tools to help automate the processes, but these can become a little watered down and over simplify the process. Certified practitioners are also available for hire to help provide independent 3rd party assessments using these and other tools. Understanding your team, and their behaviours, and knowing them all on a personal level are all vital in successfully progressing any project. But above all, strong leadership is what makes the difference (see Chapter 1).

Project Team Meetings

We have all heard the old business jokes about 'feeling lonely? Have a meeting!' and heard people say what a waste of time meetings are, 'I just want to get on with my job'. Whilst it's true that we can have too many meetings, too frequently and ineffectively, meetings are a critical part of business, they are critical communication forums, where everyone can be brought up to speed with need to know information, and critical decisions to progress the business can be made by the relevant group. So learning to manage meetings in a structured and time efficient way is a vital skill for TTIP. The project leader should always have a clear purpose when holding a meeting and aim for efficiency in every meeting held. The Phase Gate process provides a natural framework and timing to project team meetings, but for all types of team meetings, I have picked up a few generic tips along the way;

1) Meeting Minutes – when I started my career, I found

meetings to be managed in a relatively organised way with a clear agenda published and my boss was a good chairman at the time, so a good start (maybe I was just lucky with the company I started with). But what was very old fashioned by today's standards were the meeting minutes. These were always an exhaustive account of what everyone had said and it was a huge task to write everything down and type it all up (and this was before the days everyone had a laptop, can you believe it?), so you wouldn't often see the minutes published until 2 or 3 weeks after the meeting. Over the years, the art of taking the minutes has got slicker and slicker, focusing on recording just the agreed actions rather than on everything discussed.

A simple technique I was taught by one of my mentors a few years ago, and which I now use at every face to face meeting is to set up 2 flip charts in the meeting room. At the top of one I write 'Action Plan' and at the top of the other I write 'Parking Lot'. I always send out the meeting agenda (including the purpose of the meeting and agenda items with timings) a few days before the meeting so everyone knows clearly what the meeting is and why we are having it, and they can come prepared with the necessary information for us to make decisions there and then.

As we work through the agenda on the day, any decisions we take we write on the 'Action Plan' in marker pen. It's important to keep your meetings interactive and participative, e.g. I prefer the person taking the action to go up and write it on the flip chart, as it helps make them feel a sense of ownership. Also, be precise about what the action is, a date it will be completed by, and who is taking responsibility to deliver the action. During any meeting there are always things which come up during discussion which were not on the agenda, and/or things which are too big or complex to be dealt with by the team in the room. These are the items that get written onto the Parking Lot. This way, big, important items don't get ignored, but there is a recognition it's going to take time to work on them and usually the need to influence some big hitters outside of the room. The Parking Lot list is reviewed at the next meeting to see if anything has changed since, and whether we can take some specific actions to start influencing these things. I have found this Action Plan/Parking Lot technique to be very efficient and very effective. No one has to waste time writing minutes after the meeting, the decisions are real time and involve the whole team at the meeting, and everyone goes away with a copy of the minutes as they all take a photo of the flipcharts with their smartphone.

2) Team Purpose – every team should have a purpose. For a Project team using the Phase Gate system, the Project Definition will clearly state what the purpose is. But if your team is meeting for a different reason, and a different purpose, then it is important that one of your first actions should be to stand up and write on a board or flip chart what the Team Purpose is. Everyone should contribute to building this to create buy in, until you finalise a simple one page document that lists why the team exists and what it is there to achieve. A simple list is all that is needed, that can be referred back to whenever the team meetings drift out of scope. You may be surprised just how long

that simple list becomes. This reinforces the need for why you have assembled the team, but if the list is particularly long, you may need to consider whether the team can really handle such a long list of things, and consider creating one or more sub-teams.

3) Team Scope (or Charter) – every team needs a clear scope to clarify the boundaries of discussions in the meetings. Use a simple flip chart approach again and simply write two columns with the headings In Scope and Out of Scope. In Scope will list all the things the team will be accountable for, whereas Out of Scope will list those items that may come up within discussion surrounding the Purpose that the team is not accountable for. For example, a purely technical team may decide that they are accountable for a new product specification, but they are not accountable for compliance to that specification, which is an operational responsibility. Setting the scope is important to avoid the team trying to take on the world and put everything right in the business.

4) Team Action Plan – setting a Team Purpose, Scope and writing action oriented Minutes all go a long way to managing a team effectively. The Phase Gate project management system will automatically overlay this discipline on a new product development project, so additional documentation is unnecessary in such project teams. Another discipline that we can learn from the Phase Gate approach that can be useful to other teams is the concept of having an overarching Team Action Plan. Building on the Purpose and Scope, to ensure a true high performing team, the other elements you need to define amongst you are; Deliverables, Success Criteria, Blockers (and

how to overcome them), plus a list of the team members and resource requirements. You may even wish to give your team a distinct name to create something more tangible and a sense of belonging. All of these will serve to really get everyone on board about why they are getting together and having meetings. This may seem like a lot of upfront work and preparation before you even launch into doing stuff, and this can make people feel uncomfortable. What I normally do is start out with the Purpose (not usually too difficult but thought provoking) and then try to explore the Scope (usually quite challenging for everyone and doesn't always get finished the first round). Then I get on with the meeting, and next time I will add an agenda item on Deliverables & Success Criteria, slowly adding other elements of the Team Action Plan in future meetings if and when I feel the team is starting to lose any coherence and needs a bit more structure.

Site Based versus Virtual Teams

One specific team management challenge for a project leader working in an international business, is how to manage a global project team over multiple time zones, particularly with respect to team meetings, which are usually held virtually. I have spent many years working with and leading global teams and this is what I have learnt;

1) Be aware of the different time zones involved – if your team spread covers less than 8 hours of time zones, then you don't really have a big issue with scheduling virtual project meetings.
    a. The real challenge begins with more than 8 hour

spreads and the most challenging situation is when your project team truly spans the globe, because there is no hiding from the fact that someone, somewhere, will be losing out when you schedule a meeting time. In the businesses I have worked, the full global spread has been the norm for me, so I have lived this problem every week for many, many years. The easiest geography is for those based in Europe, because you will be right in the middle of the time zone spread and can attend meetings midday. The challenge comes for those at the extremes. I was regularly pulling together teams with people in US East Coast and Adelaide, Australia, and sometimes even US West Coast. That's over 18 hours of time zones to schedule around. Some of the most challenging calls I have ever arranged have been when I was in Hawaii (GMT -10), trying to get my head around everyone's time zone around the world. That can be a mind bending experience. And don't assume that just because you are flying every other week, having to deal with constant time zone jumps, that all your team members are as well. For those team members that don't normally travel internationally, the time zone issue does not naturally enter their heads. Another challenge you discover when scheduling virtual international meetings is those peculiar parts of the world that have half hour time zones, like Adelaide (GMT+9:30) and India (GMT+5:30). Yes, your Outlook scheduling tool adjusts everything automatically, but you still have to understand what effect your meeting timing has on the

individuals involved. If you live international travel with your job day in and day out, it is the first thing that enters your head.
b. I have read advice that suggests sharing the burden of international meeting timings by cycling regular meetings between morning, afternoon and evening calls. Whilst this sounds a good idea, my experience is that people actually prefer routine and a regular schedule for meetings, rather than keep chopping and changing. My Adelaide colleagues were used to having all their calls late at night because that's the only way they could get to talk to their US colleagues, so they were already working a schedule that naturally fit late night calls. Also, some people are naturally early birds and some are naturally night owls, and learning about your team really helps to work around their preferences in this way.
c. If you work in a truly global business, there is no getting around that you will be taking calls at odd times. And therefore it is understood that meeting times will occasionally be inconvenient for some people, such that they cannot attend, such as in the middle of the night. I have had people stay up all night to take some calls (I've done it myself), but how different is this to getting up at 3am to get to the airport for an early flight? Is that acceptable? The challenges of meeting scheduling can only be resolved so far, whether someone chooses to attend at inconvenient times becomes a matter of personal choice. Flexibility is the key, there is certainly no need or expectation for people to work 24/7, and

so in international business, flexibility in employees' working days is becoming normality.

2) Be aware of public holidays – one thing I have learnt in scheduling global team calls and physical meetings is that it always seems to be a public holiday somewhere in the world. You can look up these holidays through various means online as a first line of action, though these can be affected by local and regional variations in some countries, but ultimately check with your team members when scheduling.
   a. I always feel bad about one big meeting I held in Singapore when I had one of my team from the US over. The meeting was on July fourth, and being a Brit it just never entered my head that July fourth is 'the 4th of July'! But equally, there were other public holidays and business commitments for other attendees in the surrounding weeks, so we just had to go ahead. I owe that guy to this day.
   b. Another experience I had in a different business was the first time I travelled to our big factory in India. I had arranged with the General Manager to visit on a date in the autumn which was convenient to my diary. I booked the flights and hotel, I travelled over and arrived at the factory, only to discover that this particular day was Diwali, a major public holiday and the single biggest religious festival for Hindus, and that the GM had got all the employees to come into work that day because I was visiting. How bad did I feel? He should have told me, I could have easily changed my visit date. But because of his culture he felt my visit was too important, and because

of my cultural naivety at that time, I didn't think to check things like public holidays. Big lesson learnt.

3) Have face to face meetings – don't keep all your team interactions in the virtual world. Team building and bonding, creating shared experiences and getting to know each other on an informal basis are vital to enhancing team performance and this is only really going to happen if you get people face to face occasionally. There are also some subjects just too complex and subtle to try to have a meaningful virtual discussion, particularly strategic ones.
    a. Chances are that some or many of the people in the team know each other through other projects or other business activities, which is a good start, but ultimately, at some point, you are all going to need to get on an airplane. For big important subjects, particularly global senior management teams, with activities that will run continuously, I tend to get people together face to face twice a year, with virtual sessions in between. For big global projects, which will have a beginning and an end, I will certainly have a face to face kick off meeting, but beyond that I will judge the frequency of the need for face to face meetings as the project progresses.
    b. When scheduling face to face meetings, you need to appreciate that international travel can be a very tiring experience for people. I have travelled internationally for 40-60% of my time for the last 20+ years, so I know the physical challenges and the personal commitment involved. I loved the travel, there is no denying it is a great feeling

walking down the road and pinching yourself, saying 'I'm in Buenos Aires, I'm in Shanghai, I'm in Singapore'. International business travel gives you a lot of life enhancing opportunities, but it can also be a life destroying opportunity given that you will be away from your spouse and family, so a delicate balance is required. As my career grew, so did the international travel. I would be regularly circumnavigating the globe and would be away from home for weeks at a time. As your business grows and there is more to do, so the travel increases. I remember one particularly crazy trip, when I was living in China at the time, where I flew from China to Europe for 2 days of meetings, then back to Asia to Bangkok for 4 days, then back to Europe for 4 days, then back to China. You need a lot of stamina for such trips. The worst trips were, when based in Europe, I would spend one week in Asia, followed immediately by 1 week in the US, the time zone jumps were crippling and I would regularly fall ill whilst in the US. Several years ago, after one particular 6 week tour of duty around the world, I had people start asking me if I was okay. I had lost a lot of weight and was looking pretty unhealthy. It turns out I had reached the point of physical exhaustion due to such a long period of poor sleep, and all those endless business dinners. I learnt a valuable lesson from that episode.

c. The number one thing I have learnt about international travel is that the single most important resource is sleep. Without enough quality sleep you cannot perform, you cannot deliver effectively the job that you travelled there to do in the first place. So schedule meeting starts to allow a little lie in time for people to catch up on jet lag, 9 or 9:30 instead of 8:30am. Some people deal with jet lag much worse than others. I remember one senior colleague who wouldn't turn up for overseas meetings until midday because he just couldn't handle the fatigue. Eventually he had to leave the business, and settled for a job without international travel. Otherwise it would have destroyed his health.

4) Run virtual meetings as effectively as possible – on the surface, running a virtual meeting over Skype should be little different to running a face to face meeting, you still need an agenda, you still need action planning, you still need time keeping, etc. Meeting frequency will be set by the pace of the project. But there are three aspects of virtual meetings that require specialist focus compared to face to face meetings;
    a. Involve everyone – when running face to face meetings it is important to try to get everyone involved, especially the naturally quieter members of the team. This is a much more challenging thing to achieve when your meeting is run over Skype. When running a meeting in English, if you have team members who have English as their second (or sometimes third) language, then the challenges for them of keeping up with the conversation face to face are amplified significantly when the meeting is virtual, and these people in particular can go silent. It is important to talk during these meetings in a slow,

methodical tone, and avoid colloquialisms. Meetings which have a mixture of face to face people, plus others calling in on speaker phone are particularly challenging, as those in the room naturally take over the conversation and speed up their speech when they get enthusiastic about a topic. So you need to pay extra attention to stopping occasionally and asking for a contribution from those on the other end of the phone. How different team members choose to contribute and interact can also be a cultural thing, so watch out for this behaviour. Video conferencing is always a better alternative to phone calls because at least there is a partial physical presence of the person in the room, but only if you can reliably action the IT, otherwise the connection issues can bring down your meeting.

b. Reliable communications – schedule the meeting agenda to expect some IT down time, because there are always connection issues to deal with. The more people dialling in, and the more countries involved, the more the bandwidth will be challenged. Even recently I have had to close down more than one Skype meeting because of this and get everyone to dial into a telephone conference number, so always have a telephone conference account as a backup to use in emergencies.

c. Use appropriate IT tools – virtual meetings can be enhanced with collaboration software to facilitate things like remote brainstorming and document sharing in real time, of which there are many products on the market, and they are always getting better. The challenge with introducing new software is that there will always be a period of learning required when it is clumsy to use for the team, and if you introduce too many new software tools, too often, then people just get confused. This is a particular challenge for older members of the team versus the younger members, who tend to be a lot more software savvy. Frequently, new software is just not used to its full potential, and the team end up only using the most basic functions of collaboration software. You really need to consider picking one or two and doing offline training on these tools, otherwise the clumsiness that ensues will quickly give them a bad name within the team and they will start to hinder the meeting flow instead of helping. This is an area that I am confident we will see some great strides in over the next few years. The difference between video conferencing today versus even 10 years ago is enormous, so I am sure we will see the same with these software collaboration tools.

Key Skills

1) Keep things simple – there are certainly a lot of steps in the Phase Gate process and a lot of forms to fill out. All very necessary to manage risk on the biggest projects, but also the reason that I do not put smaller projects through this whole system, and just use a one page project tracker spreadsheet, to reduce the administrative burden of such projects to manageable levels. And whether a project uses a single project tracker or the full Phase Gate system,

remember to keep things as simple as possible. Documents and checklists should not go over one page. Not all checklist criteria are relevant to every project and not every project is big enough to justify lots of time consuming filling in of all of the spreadsheets, so make some sensible management judgements (see Chapter 4 – First Principles), all these processes should be there to help you, not to put administrative barriers in front of you. If you feel you are spending too much time form filling then there is probably something wrong and you should stop and think about your process. But having said that, it is also important not to skip Phases or Gates in the process. It is right to make the documentation for each as simple and easy to use as possible, but do not miss them out or you will lose the benefit of the disciplined approach and increase the risk of not achieving the project objectives. If, as the project leader, you are seen to start taking shortcuts with the process, then your team members will start to not take the process seriously, and before you know it, you will start to have team members missing gate meetings.

2) Keep things relevant – the process of TTIP is long. For big projects that go through the whole Phase Gate system, the project will likely take several years from inception to completion. It takes stamina to continue plugging away at the goal for all that time and for a project leader it takes strong leadership to bring the project team with you down that long path. Many times during that process it is easy to lose sight of what you set out to achieve, that is why the Project Definition and supporting documents are so important, But it is equally important that once they

are completed, you don't just treat them as another box ticking Gate exercise to get through the company's process. It is important you don't just put them in a drawer and move on. You need to bring these documents out frequently during project meetings and discussions and keep referring to them to maintain focus. And on the external side of the project, you and your team should continue to visit relevant customers constantly throughout the life of the project, working with them to understand real operating conditions. Do not just take your visiting salesmen's or your technician's assumed understanding, they both may have a part of the picture from different points of view, but only the consumer actually has the real picture. It is important throughout the project that you learn to 'keep things relevant', so the project does not drift. So form both the internal and external viewpoints, and 'check, check, check' frequently for continuing relevance.

3) Sell your project – another key skill you need to learn that will support you well throughout the whole project is 'how to sell your project'. There will be many formal occasions throughout the duration of the project where you will need to stand up and talk about your project (the initial project proposal pitch, project updates, gate meeting updates, senior management meeting updates, etc.) and there will be countless informal opportunities to talk about your project to people throughout your organisation. The ability to communicate effectively during these occasions is really important, not only for the good of the project, but also for your own career. For a technologically based new product and new business opportunity, the ability to explain the technology

simply and effectively in ways that non-technologists can understand (remember the 'stigma of technology' and the 'jargon' barriers from Chapter 2) is paramount. It is very easy for the project team and project leader to get wrapped up in the interesting science and technology that's going on in the project, but my advice is leave all that for your technical project meetings. To keep your project alive, keep it funded and keep it on the table of the Executive, you need to continually sell your project and remind people why we are doing it, what's the potential reward, what are the timescales, target customers, etc. Remember that this is a business, technology is a means to an end and that end is profit. Most non-technical executives are not interested in the technology, and if you start talking technology their eyes will glaze over and you will lose them immediately. They are not interested in what it is, they are interested in what it does and what it can do for their customers and their business. So focus on the benefits, the benefits for the customers and the benefits for the business. Any project leader will need to continuously and regularly sell the concept and win over stakeholders and influencers to keep their project on the business's agenda. If your project is not at the top table, it will not get talked about, it will not get the resources and backing and you will struggle to make progress. A key skill is learning how to explain the technology in simple laymen's terms. Use simple words, don't constantly bombard your audience with jargon. If you keep using jargon, the Executive will latch on to this and start using the same jargon, which will only serve to perpetuate the 'jargon' barrier. Reinforce the simple terminology, don't be afraid to keep reminding people when they use jargon or old fashioned terminology from the business that you want to stamp out. And always remember during your presentations to focus on 'what it does, not what it is'. Remember the 'dumbing down' barrier from Chapter 2? Don't allow your audience to dumb down your project or new product, or your project can become the subject of jokes and you will lose credibility.

CHAPTER 6

JUGGLING ALL THE BALLS – THE ART OF PORTFOLIO MANAGEMENT

In any business of any scale, there will be multiple new product and new business development projects running at the same time, even on one site. If you are a small group of sites or a global multi-national, your portfolio of projects can run into hundreds, and in many cases thousands. And so, an important skill required for 'Transforming Technology into Profit' is that of managing the whole portfolio of projects. If you do not have someone in your organisation looking over the whole portfolio, and using some kind of process to make sense of it all, you will likely be duplicating and wasting resources, lack clarity on priorities, and miss the bigger opportunities that collaboration can bring. Most importantly, your project teams may not be aligned with your business strategy and all your efforts may not be contributing towards it. So a

Portfolio Manager is essential. This role is often done by the Technology Director, Business Development Director or Chief Technology Officer, but may be a standalone role reporting into one of these positions, if the size of the business justifies it. The skills and approach of project portfolio management are very different to those of managing the individual projects themselves. In portfolio management, prioritisation is key. The portfolio manager cannot be sucked into all the projects, you need to spend your time supporting the big ones (usually as a Sponsor and Gatekeeper) and making sure these deliver. These are the ones that are going to make a big difference to your business. In one of my previous roles as CTO, we had over 1200 projects in our global new business and new product development portfolio. But I always maintained, and regularly updated, a Top 10 list, both globally and regionally, so I knew where I should focus my efforts when I was travelling around the business and visiting customers.

What is Portfolio Management?

Portfolio management can be as simple as maintaining a list of your ongoing projects or presenting a simple overview of projects versus progress (see Chart below). A simple project list should include details similar to the Ideas List criteria (Chapter 3), covering Strategic, Technical and Resource information but with more hard detail rather than Yes/No dropdown boxes, particularly on the market data and financials (e.g. Addressable Market size, Potential Annual Sales Value, EBITA, Cumulative Project Spend, Capital Spend, etc.), as more facts are known about the projects and commercial opportunities by this stage. The projects should be ranked to keep visibility of project priorities, and there are various ways to look at this, e.g.

Technical Feasibility versus Addressable Market Size, Probability of Success versus EBITA, etc., usually best viewed by plotting a few graphs to get a feel for how the whole portfolio maps out across these axes. But as the project list grows, so will the complexity and sophistication of the tools you need to use to manage the list effectively. Even for a small list, there are fundamental questions that you will need to find answers to in order to decide which projects are more important than others and where you should focus your resources.

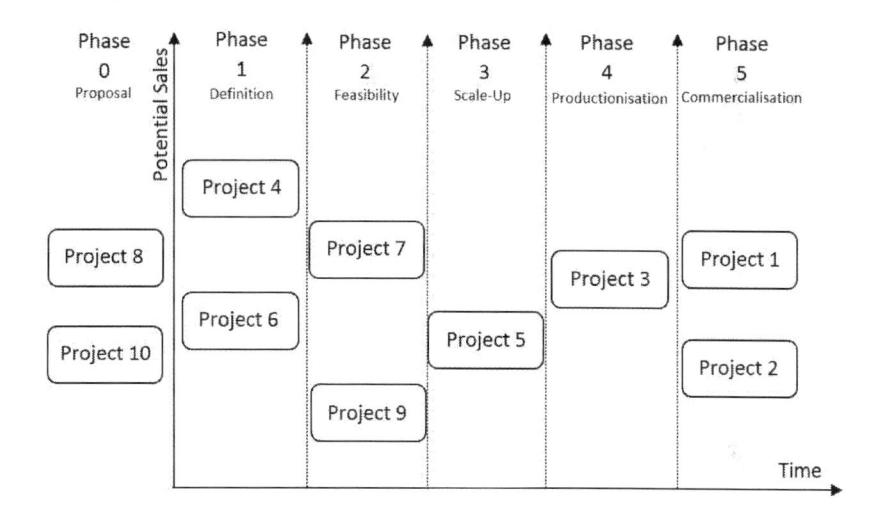

Why is Portfolio Management Important?

In my earliest attempts at managing project portfolios, I was working in businesses where new product development and new business development were considered two different things. The former was the reserve of the R&D department and the latter of the sales department. Working in technologically based industries, I discovered over time that there was much more subtlety and complexity to sales activities than just selling existing or new products to existing or new customers, and that business development at its most successful was a truly collaborative exercise (see Chapter 1). This concept can be better understood by considering the increasing levels of technical complexity and 'newness' in new products and technologies under development described in Chapter 1 (Technology Platforms – Products – Solutions – Systems), versus Customers in terms of the 'Applications' within which your products need to perform.

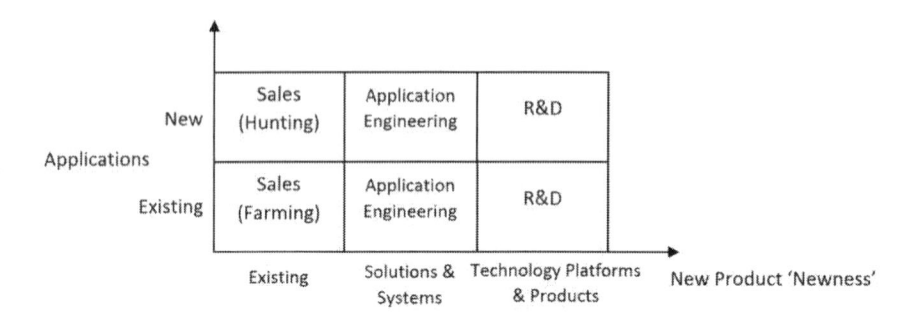

Applications	Existing	Solutions & Systems	Technology Platforms & Products
New	Sales (Hunting)	Application Engineering	R&D
Existing	Sales (Farming)	Application Engineering	R&D

(x-axis: New Product 'Newness')

As the 'Newness' of the technology behind the new products you are developing (be they Technology Platforms, Products, Solutions or Systems) increases, then the skill set required to deliver the project changes. Fundamentally new technology platforms and products need deep technical skills. Solutions and Systems are usually design challenges, and may be utilising combinations of existing (or new + existing) products to produce a new functionality. This still produces a new product for sale to customers, but it does not necessarily require deep technical skills to develop, and so this is an Application Engineering task. For new applications with existing products (be they at existing or new customers), a technology based approach is still required, because the existing products need to perform under new working conditions and in new environments, pushing the boundaries of what the product can do, so the sales person still needs Technical and Application Engineering support to convince the customer, manage the trials and sell the product.

In trying to manage this spread of project types, the sales team traditionally managed the pure Sales activities and the R&D team managed the R&D projects, but what I observed was that the big chunk of Application Engineering projects in the middle often did not easily have a home. Some of them were managed by the sales team, some by R&D and some just flapped about in their own existence, not covered by either group. This was a result of the lack of clarity of what Application Engineering really was and where it should sit within an organisational structure. Different businesses I worked with had different legacy views on this and hence had different ways of managing it site to site. This links back to the importance of recognising Application Engineering as a functional interface (see Chapter 1).

What I came to realise, was that all these projects are different aspects of the same thing. They are all new business development projects. They are all trying to achieve the same thing, grow the business, and the only reason I could see that they were managed in separate ways was the legacy of a silo organisational structure. So if a business truly wants to have full visibility of all of its technologically based new business opportunities, and be in control of them, then they need one system that unifies all their New Business Opportunities, combining all of their Application Engineering, R&D and Sales Hunting based opportunities. So when I refer to New Business Development throughout this book, I am talking about the full range of opportunities based on Application Engineering, R&D and Sales Hunting activities, I am not including new sales from existing products in existing applications (otherwise known as 'Farming'), I leave that firmly in the domain of the sales team.

It is important to recognise that new business development is only one part of a company's future potential sales growth. The other three parts are sales growth from existing products, mergers & acquisitions and inflation. How you intend to manage the balance between new business development, sales growth and M&A in terms of growth targets is something which should be addressed by your business strategy.

Having one single, unified new business development portfolio in your business delivers a number of benefits. It gives senior management clear visibility of all that is going on around the business and a mechanism to review these activities at Executive meetings, to set targets, monitor progress, make decisions, agree priorities and plan for the future. It is a critical tool in driving a key aspect of your business strategy and helps with resource planning and deployment. It provides a means for communication of new business opportunities around the business and helps to identify opportunities for collaboration. It provides the sales team with a standardised process to better manage their own pipeline, and a crystal ball to forecast their sales into the future. Having one standard tool improves data quality and reduces errors and ensures standardised metrics to assess and communicate your portfolio. The quantity of data involved in managing a portfolio of hundreds or thousands of projects is vast. Having a good new business development portfolio tool provides the structure to make sense of this complexity.

What does a Portfolio Management System look like?

There are plenty of different formats for a new business development portfolio management tool, but at their most basic level they will all start with some form of database, be it a simple spreadsheet, an Access-style database or a full CRM based system. Overlaying the database will be analytical tools, charts and tables, and overlaying that there may be visualisation tools to aid understanding and communication of the output. A modern system will provide a standardised but customisable dashboard, with graphical representation of the pipeline with charts, tables & structured analysis that allows the sales team to cut and paste data into their reports and presentations.

Before you can build a portfolio management tool, you need to agree a set of rules for the system, to define what will be included and what will not. For example, it is normal in capturing new business development projects that these should reflect only 3rd Party sales projects. If you are a large, multi-site group, there will likely be intercompany project activity, some of which will be necessary to deliver the ultimate 3rd party business, but this does not grow your business, this only moves money around your group, so it is important that your rules clearly state; '3rd Party sales projects only'. This can create problems with those project owners in charge of the intercompany projects because they complain that they don't get recognition for all the work they are doing. This reflects a site versus group cultural issue in your business that needs addressing.

For each new business development project, you will need to collect a standardised, basic set of information, which will form the data that are entered into your portfolio tool. For a short list of projects you might choose to gather and enter this information yourself, but as the list grows you will need to appoint someone to enter the data, though ultimately, when the list grows too long, the project owners themselves really need to be entering the data into the system. This reinforces ownership to them and ensures everyone is actively using the portfolio tool. If they have to open the portfolio system to enter their data, then they are more likely to look at their dashboard and use the system.

Typical information that you should collect for each project is listed below. It should be noted that with a reasonably sophisticated CRM system, some of these categories can be auto-generated and will not require physical data entry. All the project information that is necessary to be collected to allow a useful level of portfolio management capability, can be categorised into 5 distinct groups as listed below, and so the system architecture and data entry fields should be organised to reflect this for ease of data entry.

1) Project Identification
    a. Project Owner – as mentioned in Chapter 5, it is absolutely critical for the success of any project that one person has clear ownership. This same person should also be the one entering the data in the portfolio system. I have worked in businesses where some project owners delegate project data entry to a junior office person, but this is always in my experience a mistake. The office person rarely knows anything about the project, and certainly not to the depth that the owner does, leading inevitably to data errors. It is also a good indicator that the project owner is not really managing the project in a structured way. I have also seen systems that nominate sales

leads and technical leads separately, which is fine, as long as the Project Owner is made crystal clear.

b. Lead Business – this is the name of the business that is taking the lead on the project, usually the one that the project owner is affiliated to or based at. This must be a required field if your business has multiple sites. Usually done as a dropdown box multiple choice field. The names can reflect how you talk about your business. Sites are often discussed in terms of the town or city they are located in, or it could be by country. Above that, you may need an additional regional category if you are a truly globalised business and need to split data by Asia-Pac, EMEA, etc. or a business division category if you are structured that way. But whichever method of naming you use, make sure to keep one consistent naming convention, i.e. don't use a mix of country names and site names, use one or the other, otherwise it can lead to confusion. Your system will have cleaner data if everyone uses the same terms for everything, e.g. everyone around the business calls the sites by the same names. Having a global management system is an excellent way to reinforce a wide range of naming conventions around your business, to reduce the complexity and confusion.

c. Currency – this must be a required field if your business has multiple sites in different countries. On a database system, this can be auto-generated by the location that is selected. Overall you will be reviewing your portfolio under one currency, usually the currency that your Head office or

Region does business in, so having real time exchange rates issued by your business for finance purposes built into your system, is an absolute necessity to ensure your system works smoothly and is up to date. In global portfolio management systems, I have found that foreign exchange errors are the most frequent source of project financial data errors. The more sophisticated your system becomes, the more you need to be looking under the hood of the system to keep it working well.
   d. Project ID Code – it is useful to assign a unique project code number to each project as this helps with tracking projects through the system and serves as an easy reference point for portfolio discussions. This can be easily auto-generated by your system, just adding a new cumulative code each time a new project is entered into the system.
   e. Project Start Date – this should be the date that the entry was first made into the system and is the trigger to generate a new Project ID code.
   f. Project Completion Date (estimated) – expected date when the project should reach 100% completion, i.e. Phase 5 (see below).
   g. Project Timescale – the system can auto-generate the anticipated project timescale based on the two previous fields, to give an expectation of how long it is likely to take to deliver this project and the expected sales potential.

2) Project Description
   a. Project Type – the new business development system we are building is built around the scope

of including all new technologically based business development activities (as detailed above). This includes Application Engineering, R&D and Sales Hunting type projects, which in turn are led by either the Sales, Application Engineering or Technology functions. As such, in order to segment the new business development portfolio to clarify ownership at the senior management level, I have learnt that it is very helpful to assign projects into one of three categories of projects – Technical, Application Engineering, and Commercial. This gives the organisation a better appreciation of how these projects differ in style and allows an often very big portfolio to be sliced up into three parts, with the functional leads taking ownership. As discussed earlier, as the Application Engineering function is an interface and doesn't normally have a discrete owner, the structure of the business will dictate whether the owner becomes the Technical or Sales lead. The 'Project Type' data field should be a drop down box with only three choices – Technical, Application Engineering or Commercial. Clear and simple category definitions are very important for users to refer to both in the live document and as part of the training package;

i. Technical Projects – Projects where the output will be a new Technology platform or a new product (see definitions Chapter 1).
ii. Application Engineering Projects – Projects where the output will be a new solution or a new system (see definitions Chapter 1).
iii. Commercial Projects – Projects where the

output will be an existing product in a new application (Sales Hunting).

In terms of the new business development project model at the start of this chapter, these three project categories can be overlaid as shown below. I have seen project definitions get ever more long and complex in an attempt to try to cover all eventualities as they arise, but this is a mistake in the long term, as all it does is serve to confuse the system user. In a large, complex business, serving multiple markets, you will need to accept that there are always unusual projects coming up that require some degree of judgement to assign the right category. It is also possible that a project may start out in one category, but as the project progresses, working more closely with the customer redirects the project in a different direction, and so the category may change, requiring a different approach by the project team. This reinforces the need for regular updates of project data by the project owner.

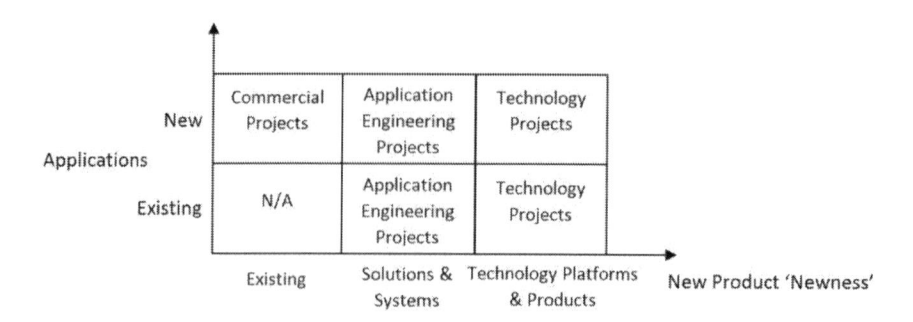

Applications		Existing	Solutions & Systems	Technology Platforms & Products
New		Commercial Projects	Application Engineering Projects	Technology Projects
Existing		N/A	Application Engineering Projects	Technology Projects

New Product 'Newness'

We can however add some more useful background to each project type to add context.

iv. Technical Projects – these will be what are traditionally considered R&D projects, and will feature more heavily in the new business portfolio management system as they progress to the later commercialisation phases of a project, as individual customers become targeted and take trials. As I explained at the start of this chapter, I have found it important to integrate these into the new business development portfolio to avoid the traditional attitude in many businesses that these are high risk projects that should be left independent in case they don't deliver. This is a big mistake. If you treat them like this they will fail. But if you lock them into your new business pipeline and link them to delivering future sales in your finance systems, then you will work these projects much harder to make them succeed. These will also tend to be the longer term, more complex projects, requiring a full Phase Gate project management approach.

v. Application Engineering Projects – these will typically be projects with a high degree of design or product bespoking and can involve existing or new products or a mixture of the two. Less 'science' is required to deliver these products, and more a working practical knowledge of how your technologies behave in real working environments. These will tend to be the medium term, medium complexity projects that require some degree of project management, but which don't need a full set of project management documentation, so a project tracker can be used.

vi. Commercial Projects – these will typically be projects that employ existing products but use them within new working environments. Technical support from R&D and Application Engineering teams will be needed to manage product trials and work with the customer on how best to use the product in the new working conditions. These will tend to be the shorter term, more simple projects, requiring only a simple Gantt chart to track progress (see chart below).

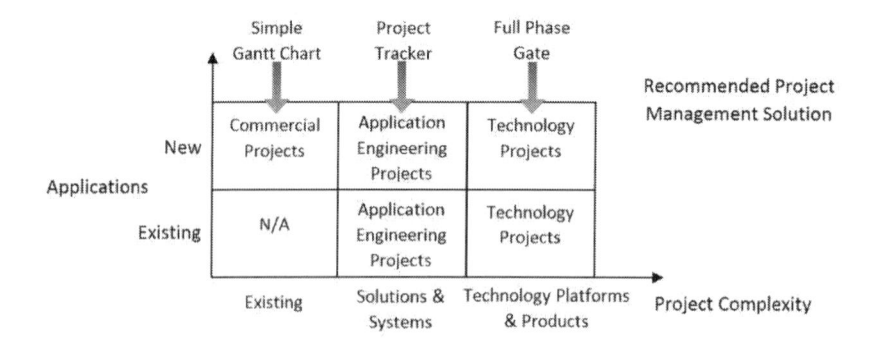

	Existing	Solutions & Systems	Technology Platforms & Products
New Applications	Commercial Projects (Simple Gantt Chart)	Application Engineering Projects (Project Tracker)	Technology Projects (Full Phase Gate)
Existing Applications	N/A	Application Engineering Projects	Technology Projects

Recommended Project Management Solution — Project Complexity →

b. Product Description – as most of your new business development projects will have some degree of new product, solution or system development, then your project product descriptions will mostly be unique to each project. The only exception will be Commercial projects where you are trying to use existing products in new applications. Therefore, this category usually works best with a dropdown box, to reinforce existing product naming conventions, but with the added capability of a free form typeable field to allow for new product types. Reinforcing rules of product naming conventions during data entry will include things like using the full official product brand rather than shortened code versions of the name. Any new description should be brief but still convey all the necessary information. If the product is manufactured at a site that is different from that named in the Lead Business category, then you may wish to add an additional field with a drop down box, to select the manufacturing site. If multiple manufacturing sites are involved, select the site that delivers the largest percentage of final sales to the project.

c. Product Group – if your business is complex enough to produce more than one type of product, then you will need to identify which product group your product is part of. This should preferably be a drop down box to limit the number of options, to avoid spelling mistakes and to get everyone using the same set of product group naming conventions. It may be that your new product is going to create a brand new product group for your company, in which case you should maintain the ability to type in a free form field description, but this will need policing to avoid too many new and unwarranted product groups appearing. If a project is bringing together more than one product to create a solution or system, then for simplicity, my experience is that it is best to select the product group here that

represents the largest percentage of the sales potential.
   d. Application Description – this should be a free form field to capture a short but clear description of how and where the new product is going to be used. It is important to keep it brief but informative.

3) Customer and Market Details
   a. New or Existing Customer – this should be a simple dropdown box with only 2 options to select. Selecting 'Existing' should trigger dropdown boxes in the next two categories for auto completion. Selecting 'New' should allow the user to create a new customer on the system, with the system assigning a new customer code.
   b. Target Customer Name – this should be the standard official customer name as listed in the sales reporting system for existing customers, selected by drop down box, or for new customers, the official legal company name should be used to create a new customer in your database. You may need to add an additional category if you have customers that are part of bigger groups, so that you can identify more clearly the total new business potential you have with the group globally. For large engineering and infrastructure projects (which would normally sit in the Application Engineering project category), these are typically put up for tender across a number of potential competing customers at the start of a project. So the customer name may change as the project progresses. Projects which target markets (e.g. big R&D projects) will have

potential across a wide range of customers and geographies. Typically such Technology projects split into multiple, targeted new business opportunities as they progress to commercialisation phase and will produce several discrete customer targeted projects.

c. Customer Number – this field should be auto generated by the selection of the existing customer name in your sales database, or auto created when creating a new customer on your system.

d. Customer Type – a drop down box to identify the customer relationship and their point in the sales channel, e.g. distributor, reseller, end user, etc.

e. Origin of Lead – this should be a drop down box indicating whether the opportunity came from a customer visit, a phone call, a web enquiry, an internal idea, etc., to analyse how projects are coming into your business.

f. Market – this field has to link to the same set of market codes used in your financial reporting and sales analysis system, otherwise you will struggle to get all the systems in your business to interface with each other. You may need a second data entry field for market segmentation if your company services a wide variety of complex markets, that each have further segmentation. Again, use the standard codes used throughout your business.

g. Competitor – you should record any known active competitor(s) on this project. This affects the Probability of Success calculation in the Project Status section. There may be more than one active competitor, so your system needs to be able to cope with that situation. If you are designing a unique, bespoke system or solution for a customer, then you may not have a direct active competitor.

4) Project Status
   a. Project Phase – I have seen many different versions of how businesses split the progress of their new business development projects into phases to try to map progress. Normally, businesses start by trying to capture every separate phase in a way that tries to cover all types of projects and end up with too many phases. As I have said several times, in a complex business, there is no one size fits all solution. If you go that way you will end up with a system that is over complex, not user friendly and is out of touch with reality. Typically, I have seen systems that try to work with 7, 8 and sometimes 10 project phases. Whilst each of these were always logical and academically correct, in reality, what I found is that when the portfolio data was being reported, people would typically group some of the phases together because the audience would find 10, 8 or even 7 phases too much to absorb and make resourcing and prioritisation decisions on. So even though there might have been good logical reason to have up to 10 phases representing different aspects of the progress of their projects, in reality the data was actually being used in groups of 4 or 5 categories. This is why I finalised on 5 project phases as the optimum for a portfolio management system,

because this represents the best compromise between how projects really progress and the way the output is actually used.

Another important observation I made over time, was that every company I worked with tried to get all their new business development projects to fit into a single common project phase system, but often, projects would appear that didn't fit the defined phases and so had to be shoe-horned in. And worse still, extra phases would be added in to account for such projects that didn't fit the system. I saw one 10 Phase system grow to become 12 phases, adding first a Phase 0, and then Phase -1. What I grew to understand was that there were projects that didn't fit the standard phase categories because new business development involves a range of different types of projects, This is where the concept of Technical Projects versus Application Engineering Projects versus Commercial Projects (or Sales Hunting) came from (see 'Project Type').

Once you realise that there are fundamentally different types of project under the lid of your new business development portfolio, then you can start to appreciate why one set of rules for project phasing cannot apply. Since we now understand that 5 Phases are the optimum number and that there are 3 types of projects at play, then it becomes clear that the three types of project need their own individual set of project phases. This is fine and not over complex, because they all still go through 5 phases, so reporting in either a consolidated or separate manner still works smoothly and the output is easily understood.

Project Phase	1	2	3	4	5
Technology	Definition	Feasibility	Scale Up	Productionisation	Commercialisation
Application Engineering	Budgetary Offer	Design	Customer Testing	Order awarded	Order supplied
Commercial	Opportunity Assessment	Commercial Offer	Product Adjustment	Order Received & Manufactured	Full Production & Invoicing

Therefore, this data entry field should be a simple drop down box where the user has to make a choice from one of the 5 project phases. Another reason for using the 5 phase approach is that the Technology projects link directly to the 5 Phases in the Phase Gate project management system, allowing project management and portfolio management systems to interface efficiently. As with some of the other categories, as a project progresses, there may be times when it has to jump back to an earlier phase, e.g. a customer trial failed and it's back to the drawing board. In cases like this, the project owner should change the project phase category accordingly. The only exception is when a project reaches phase 5. At that point it is 100% complete and the system will treat it accordingly.

b. Project Stalled – this should be a simple Yes or No selection in the data entry field, and can be enhanced with conditional formatting and colour coding to highlight stalled projects in red, and those on track in green.

c. Probability of Success – I have explored several methods of calculating probability of success of a project over the years, based on formulae drawing project data from the database. Each one became more complicated than the last as new projects and new data highlighted limitations in the model. What I eventually settled on as the best method was the most simple. I recommend that your probability of success is a simple auto-generated field based on project phase versus competitor activity. Using the 5 project phases described above, a project at Phase 1 will have 20% probability of success, at Phase 2 a 40% probability of success, at Phase 3, 60%, at Phase 4, 80%, and so on. If a competitor is present (entered into the Competitor field) then the probability at each phase is halved, and if two competitors are present, then it is halved again. This keeps things realistic and requires no direct judgement on the part of the project owner when inputting data.

    d. Date of last data entry – this should be an auto-generated field indicating the last time the project data was updated. This is useful for policing the system and checking that project owners are using the system and keeping project information up to date. Sophisticated systems can also be set up to trigger reminders to project owners (and their managers) that they haven't used the system in a while (a time limit needs to be decided that's relevant to your business).

5) Financial Data
    a. Total Annual Sales Potential – if this project goes to successful completion, what is the maximum annual sales value it could generate for the business? This is one of the most fundamental data fields for a new business development

project, which receives a lot of attention by management. Some systems I have seen apply a threshold value to the total annual sales potential to avoid filling up the system with lots of very small projects. There is some logic to this, but large groups have a tendency to apply the same threshold value across the whole company. The effect of this is that the smaller companies of the group don't have many (if any) projects on the system as their new business opportunities are too small to be above the threshold and so cannot or do not use the system. This is the result of having a corporate, top down approach to new business development. Although this might produce a useful system for the central marketing team to analyse future business potential for the company, it can result in a feeling around the business that the system is just a form filling exercise for the corporate headquarters, resulting in disenchantment and lack of commitment. What I have found best, is to let each site assign their own threshold value, such that they can use the system effectively for their own business. Whilst this does result in a database with lots more smaller projects, a sophisticated CRM system can be set up to allow the user to filter out projects below certain values, effectively assigning a threshold value that is relevant to whomever is mining the data, producing output relevant and useful at the site, regional, GBU or corporate level as required. Flexibility and thinking about the system from the point of view of all users around the business are the keys to success here.

b. Sales Forecast by Quarter (and by year) – for sales forecasting purposes, it is useful to have the total sales potential field broken down by quarter, to understand how sales are expected to ramp throughout the current year, and by current and subsequent years, for future visibility. This also helps to set expectations for when the total potential of the project might be reached, is it next year or 5 years from now? For further integration, these data can also be linked to sales targets in your sales management or CRM system and linked to sales people's bonuses.

c. Total Estimated Customer Spend – it is very useful to understand what share of a customer's spending power you believe you are addressing with your project, as this helps the business understand overall market size, its market share, and its capacity for future growth, plus it helps the sales team plan its approach.

d. Total 'Through' % Gross Margin – this needs to be 'through' margin to reflect the intercompany contribution that will be part of your projects if you are a group of businesses. If your business strategy is aiming for profit growth then you can set a threshold margin here to ensure that no project is worked on that would dilute your overall margin, so that all new business development projects in the system are contributing towards profitable growth, not just sales growth.

e. Capex required (value) – some projects are going to need capital expenditure to build extra production capacity, or build a completely new production process. At the early stage of a

project it is challenging to have any real foresight about how large this might be, so I always take this data field with a pinch of salt, but it's important to have something in there so the business is not under any illusion that some capex requirement is coming down the line if this project is successful.
f. Capex required (date) – the system also needs a timeframe for when the capex investment is likely to be required, to aid future capex planning.

Beyond these entry level data categories, there will likely be specific nuances of your business that require some of these to be tailored to reflect how your business runs and the nature of the markets within which you play. You will also need to decide which of these data fields you want to make mandatory and which you will allow some flexibility in input, particularly in the earlier stages of data input, e.g. % gross margin may not be so clear in the early stages of the project, particularly if it is a new product requiring a new production process, that is not yet costed out, but as it progresses it should become a mandatory field. Also, it is important to appreciate that whilst each dataset for each project forms a snapshot of what the whole project is about, where it's heading, and its current state of progress, this should not be considered as a suitable means of managing a project. This is not a project management tool (see Chapter 4), and it would be a mistake for project owners to use it in this way. It is not a substitute for proper project management tools and techniques, rather the data in the portfolio management system should form an output from the project management system, and in this way there is much scope for the two systems in your business to interface.

One particular challenge you will face if you want to set up a new business development portfolio management system in a global business is all the different languages involved. You will presumably be aiming to output the top level management summary in the language that drives your business, usually English if you are a Western company, or Chinese if you are a Chinese multi-national, but what about the input? If you have multiple sites in multiple international locations, then do you insist that they all input in the standard company language? e.g. all input in English? Whilst this is possible to insist, and takes out a level of complexity in how the system has to work, it guarantees you a level of errors that will creep in, as Chinglish, Singlish, and other local nuances, inevitably find their way into the data set. Better to let users input in local languages, or at least the cluster dominant languages, though this means you will need to build quite a sophisticated system that can handle different character sets and translations.

The long list of project categories listed above will all form data entry fields in your system, but what about output? What will your system do with all this information, and how will you display and report it? For this you will need to construct a dashboard. To assist with regular review of the new business development pipeline around the business, your system needs to have an easy to read and easy to use reporting dashboard, detailing all the Key Performance Indicators and charts needed by the business to help management both understand and make positive decisions to help progress. In any sophisticated CRM database, the dashboard can be configured to individual and group users, so that a site management team only has to see data relevant to its site, and a regional management team only needs to see data relevant to its region, etc. Although it should also be configured with the flexibility to drill down and across the data of other group businesses and sites as required by users. There can be considerations of levels of security versus data access across a business, but in reality, if you truly want to encourage collaboration, you need to allow full data access across the business. The only exception would be if there were any new business projects involving technologies subject to export controls, and other jurisdictional restrictions, such as defence and military work, e.g. ITAR in the US (International Traffic in Arms Regulations). If your business works in these areas, you will need a fully partitioned system to cope with this or even a standalone, isolated database with restricted access to approved individuals.

Whatever your scenario, any dashboard needs to feature a set of standard charts, tables and data, to provide a quick and accurate overview of the state of the new business development pipeline. Typical data displayed will include metrics that monitor the health of your new business pipeline (e.g. % conversion rate, time to convert, total size of pipeline, % new product sales, etc.), and analytical tools that provide an overview of the pipeline itself (e.g. split of projects by phase, total sales potential by year, sales potential by market, sales potential by product group, top ten projects, top ten customers, etc.). It is important not to over complicate the dashboard, by restricting the number of charts and tables to just a handful, so you will need to decide which are the most relevant data to display and how best to interpret and action the output based on your business strategy. The metrics section of your dashboard should display the current status of your metrics and a graph of how they have changed with time. This will give you an immediate view of whether your new business development activities are improving or not, e.g. is your % conversion rate increasing over time? Is your time to convert projects reducing? Is your % new product sales increasing? Are you growing the total pipeline? These are all very important measures of the health of your new business pipeline and should be a regular part of your senior management reviews and a key source of actions to make further improvements or correct metrics that are going the wrong way.

Tips for Building a Portfolio Management System

Whilst designing new business opportunity portfolio systems, there have been several important lessons I learnt along the way;

1) Treat the building of the system as a project – create a project team incorporating key people from around the business, a mixture of end users and administrators, senior and junior roles. For a companywide system, it is also vital that you have a member of the executive as sponsor to ensure commitment from the very top, otherwise you will have a big challenge during implementation. Build a project definition (what are you trying to achieve?), targets (when do you know you've achieved it?), a plan (how are you going to achieve it?) and run meetings regularly to track progress.
2) Start simple – start with a spreadsheet based system, work through the system and debug, and get the processes working right first before you go to a full IT database or CRM solution. Use dropdown boxes as much as possible to reinforce product naming conventions, business site names, market codes, etc. and avoid spelling mistakes. Use the same naming conventions used throughout your other business

systems (e.g. finance systems, sales reporting, etc.) to ensure commonality of language and to optimise cross-communication between systems. Starting with a spreadsheet is an easy starting point to build the system, but because there are so many items to capture for each project, the spreadsheet can end up with many, many columns (there can be over 40 if you need all of the data points referred to above) making it clunky to use, as it requires a lot of scrolling across for data entry. It also requires a lot of manual collation regionally and globally. All of this makes for an unpopular system amongst users, so if you start with a spreadsheet, make sure you view this as only a starting point, not the end point. Ultimately, you should be heading for a fully integrated CRM database solution. This is much more user friendly for data entry and easier to generate clear and useful dashboards, but also has the capability of exporting a dataset to a spreadsheet if an individual user wants to do further analysis.

3) Manage the experts – I learnt that for IT projects, don't give them to IT people to run, because in reality, they are not IT projects, they are business process projects that utilise IT as a means to implement them. So whenever I start a major process improvement project that will require an IT solution, I do not initially include anyone from IT, because I discovered early on that often the IT expert will simply tell you why you 'can't do that', or 'that will be difficult', and put barriers up in the project before it has even started. I always now firstly form a team from people who understand the business process, both administrators and users, people who know the pitfalls and challenges of the current system, and

together we build the ideal system that is right for the business. Only then do I bring the IT expert into the team and start working together on designing the architecture, implementing the system around the business and cascading training to all end users. It is the same thing as if your new product development process is led by a technical expert, they also view the challenge from the point of view of existing technology and say things like, 'that can't be done', 'that will be very difficult', etc., and impose boundaries on a project before the proposal has even been formed. Experts need to be managed carefully early on in the inception of a project and then brought in at the right time.

4) Communicate progress – keep the business and the end users (those who will actually be using it) informed as the system is being built. Explain what your team is doing, why you are doing it, what the benefit will be to them and the business and give updates on progress and the expected go live date. Get regular feedback on the nature of the data required and the types of information that will be requested, so that there are no surprises when it comes to the go live date.

5) System Administration versus Project Ownership – when you set up and roll out a companywide system for managing the new business project portfolio, I have observed some confusion surrounding ownership. If someone is appointed as responsible for the new business development system, the rest of the business behaves as if this person own all the projects. On the flip side, the project owners can feel some loss of control and hence some loss of ownership. It is therefore very important to clarify

the role of everyone in the process and to reinforce that the project owners are still 100% the project owners. I try to address this by defining people who are responsible for the system as 'system administrators'. Ownership and accountability for the projects must lie with the individual businesses, regions and project owners. The administrators simply gather the data, do the analysis and report the results. Management then review and make decisions with the results.

6) System launch – once your new system is built and debugged well enough, you will need an official go live date to communicate to everyone in the business when you will be transitioning to the new system. This is particularly important if your system is replacing an existing one of some kind. Note that I said debugged 'well enough'. You can carry on debugging forever, you will still find little issues now and again, but at some point you need to launch and let it out into the real world. Only then will further user issues arise, which, provided you have put in place ongoing system support, you can easily fix as you go. This has to be a dynamic system which you work to continuously improve.

7) Training and ongoing system support – in parallel to building and launching the IT aspect of the new business development system, you also need to be creating a training package, with supporting documentation and a roll out plan. It is no good building a clever, effective system if your users don't know how to enter data, look at and interpret their dashboard, etc. Even the act of logging onto any new system needs to be explained clearly to people. If your system is not easy to access, not easy to navigate

and not easy to use, then it will fail, as people will not become adopters. There is some element you can introduce to some extent of forcing people to use it by linking different systems up, so they need the system data to feed other things they are using, e.g. sales planning, but this will not make it popular unless you address the ease of use and provide adequate training. The training package should include a standard user manual and a training presentation, which can then be cascaded through the organisation in a standardised way, via face to face and online sessions as appropriate, right down to local site level. Each division or region needs to have a training co-ordinator nominated, who is responsible for ensuring that all people are trained and can act as the primary contact for any subsequent queries. Also, if you want your top management involved, then make sure you train them as well, so they are fully aware of the system, as some of them will be users in the sense of accessing the overall dashboard. Once the initial training program has gone through the whole organisation, the project team should continue to act as the steering committee for the system. The steering committee's role is to police the system, listen to and action feedback from users, continue to make improvements and organise training of any new employees. At the go live date, there will be the one off burden of data entry to populate the database for all projects, or alternatively there may be a transition of data from an existing system to the new system, either way, extra support must be available to help users through this transition and to double check data.

Tips for Managing a Portfolio Management System

1) Communicate – it is important to communicate to all users that the system is a living, dynamic document. It will be changing constantly as data are added and modified. In particular, some people get nervous about when to first enter their project into the system, because they don't have all the information yet to fill out all the columns or data entry fields, e.g. final customer not yet known, full sales potential unclear, etc. For the system to be as useful as possible to the business, it is important that these projects are included as early as possible with as much information as is available or best guess. The project owners need to be constantly encouraged to update their project data as the project progresses and they gain better clarity on the unknowns and best guesses from their earlier data entry, to ensure the quality of information improves over time.

2) Police the system – you need to be policing the system constantly, checking for anomalies. Sometimes someone puts a sales potential in that is just crazily big, ten or a hundred times bigger than the next biggest opportunity. This generally elevates the project right up to the top ten in your project portfolio, out of nowhere. If you review the portfolio regularly, you will spot this immediately in the system, which prompts you to dig in and start asking questions. Usually it is just a data entry error or a typo, e.g. typing in 100 instead of 10. For multi-national project systems, this situation can be the result of a foreign exchange error, e.g. the number was typed in as Korean Won but displayed as US$, big difference! The steering committee is the best

forum to raise anomalies and the best group of people to be looking for them. Not only does this keep your data real and relevant, it also helps to debug and continuously improve the system.

3) Integration – for full acceptance of the system companywide, you should aim for full integration of your portfolio management system into the business, by linking it with existing project management tools and with all other management systems present in your business, e.g. sales reporting, financial controls, invoicing, manufacturing scheduling, purchasing and inventory control, etc. This is a lot of work to do, but if it remains a standalone system, it will always be a little bit clunky to use, as end users will need to move data manually from one system to another. You should aim to integrate the system at both the IT level, with communication links between systems, and at the user level, with use of the same terminology, code systems, etc., as used in the other management systems. Without full integration, there is always a danger that the portfolio management system sits outside the day to day running of the business, which leads to a 'hidden projects' culture (see item 6 below). The most sophisticated businesses should have full integration of all their business management tools, with one system feeding into another, with no separate standalone systems. I have never yet worked in a business that has achieved this utopia, but that should always be the ultimate end point for business management system development.

4) Review the output regularly – for any portfolio management tool to deliver what it is designed to do, the output must be reported and reviewed regularly

at senior management meetings. The new business opportunity portfolio should be a regular agenda item at the site, regional, GBU and global level. Each level of management should be reviewing their particular dashboard, keeping up to date with the priority projects, and offering the necessary support to unblock any barriers to progress through resource and investment decisions. If you want your projects to be a success, they must be highly visible and a subject of regular discussion at management and board meetings, otherwise you will struggle to get the resources needed to deliver them.

5) Pet projects – every business and every board always has strong individuals, who have strong views on things, and new business development projects are no different. You will frequently have to deal with board or portfolio management committees where each person has their own pet project and will continue to push it at every opportunity. To address this you need two things, 1) an effective portfolio management process and 2) the skills to manage the backroom politics outside the meeting itself, e.g. during meeting breaks, during business dinners, in the bar afterwards, etc.

6) Hidden projects – another issue you will discover is that people often don't want to put their project in to the system because they think it will get too much attention from management and they will have management jumping all over them. They don't want the interference. There are also people who act like they exist outside the rest of the company's systems, these are typically entrepreneurial types, who struggle to work within a big corporate structure with all of its rules, but who are invaluable in generating new

business as they are the true hunters. These are challenging situations to manage. To truly understand your opportunity pipeline, you need all the opportunities in the system. If these hidden projects have big sales potential associated with them, then they will really affect the portfolio, seriously under reporting your future business potential and leading to misinformed and potentially bad decisions to be made regarding resource deployment. So how do you persuade people to input their information? My experience is that you need to constantly act as the champion for the system, explaining its value to people frequently, encouraging users, getting feedback from them, etc. For the entrepreneurs, it's best to get someone to work alongside them to capture the data entry because the entrepreneur type of person rarely wants to (or is good at) data entry type exercises. You also need to keep your ear to the ground to make sure you hear about these big projects in the first place.

I have implemented the portfolio management tools described in this chapter successfully in several businesses, and in each case we made significant improvements in the health of the new business portfolio, in many cases doubling the total sales pipeline, doubling conversion rate, and more than doubling % new product sales. Typically, it takes between 1 and 2 years to reach this level of improvement, depending on the scale and complexity of the business and the level of commitment from senior management.

Intellectual Property Portfolio Management

If your business is busy working to generate new technologies and new products, then you will also be generating Intellectual Property (see Chapter 4). As your portfolio of IP grows, then so will your need to have a methodical approach to managing your portfolio. This is an additional, specialist layer of portfolio management that is worth covering in this chapter, as it is often forgotten about or put to one side as a company often does not have the specialist skills to deal with. Management of the full IP portfolio is another responsibility that I prefer to give to the Innovation Council (see Chapter 3). By full IP portfolio, I am referring not only to patents, but also to trademarks & trade secrets, all of which need top down management to be of commercial value to the business.

Managing your IP portfolio can start as easily as having a simple list of all active IP in your business, containing details of the patents, trademarks, country coverage, grant dates, renewal dates and fees, etc. Maintaining such a spreadsheet, keeping it up to date and making renewal decisions, is not always however an easy task. For a start, there needs to be one person with the clear responsibility in your business to manage this. This is a particular challenge if you work in a group of businesses, especially a multi-national. Groups of businesses usually expand through acquisition over long periods, requiring regular integration of newly acquired businesses into the Group culture and processes. Any business the group acquires will usually come with its own legacy IP. Depending on how good your acquisition integration process is, their legacy IP may or may not come to your attention and may or may not get integrated into your central IP spreadsheet. If your business suffers from inadequate integration of acquisitions, and many do, then this makes controlling a portfolio of IP a real challenge. The new sites will also have their own local IP legal contacts, so you need to make decisions about whether to continue using these or bring in your own company IP support. Depending on the culture in your business, and the level of autonomy they want local sites to have versus the corporate centre, this may not just be a one-time issue to deal with because unless someone tells them any different, the local site are just going to carry on managing their own IP, filing their own local patents, in isolation, without reference to the central IP function.

There is a particular challenge for global companies which have manufacturing businesses and Joint Ventures in China. In China, many regional and provincial governments have a system of tax incentives for companies that can meet criteria for 'High Tech' status. One of the criteria is based on how many patents a company files. The tax incentives can be significant, saving 10% on corporate taxes. The result of this is that, if not properly managed, you have your local Chinese companies filing patents just to get the tax benefits. The patents may result in getting the tax incentives so there can certainly be value in proceeding, but it can be at the expense of public disclosure of information that the group company would prefer to remain secret. A balance needs to be drawn which can only be achieved if the local Chinese company is in the loop of the global IP management process.

With acquisitions, may also come competing brands and their associated trademarks, particularly if the acquisition was to buy market share. This requires commercial decisions, for each country and region, about whether you want to keep more than one brand active in a market and the supporting distributors and channels to market. These are all purely commercial decisions, but too often in businesses, the management of the IP portfolio is handled by the technical lead. This is why I prefer IP to be part of the scope of the Innovation Council.

Maintaining an overall IP spreadsheet and frequently reviewing the whole portfolio, gives you a great opportunity to add value to your business. The spreadsheet should include the due dates for all active patent and trademark renewals, along with the estimated costs. For historical IP, there may well be local processes already in place to automatically renew. So it is important to review the portfolio every few months and action any new decisions you make. When I have worked in large groups of companies, I have always been surprised by how many trademarks, representing old, redundant brands are still active, and in countries where the business no longer sells. This offers plenty of scope for saving money by cancelling automatic renewals. Your business may be investing considerable monies into IP, so like any resource, you need to be making sure that money is invested wisely.

How effectively your IP management is working and how well it is contributing to your business can be monitored in a number of ways. You may choose to track the value of sales protected by IP (this should be increasing if this is an objective in your IP strategy) or if you want to be more targeted, the value of sales split by defensive, aggressive and growth patents. Spreading your patent portfolio broadly across the range of Utility Patent categories (composition, form, functionality, structure and application) is also a way of adding strength to your IP patent portfolio, as you are less dependent on one form of protection, and also illustrating that your IP strategy is working to help you target your decisions appropriately for different market situations. Alternatively, you can monitor the increase in profit margins associated with IP. You can also monitor IP linked to the number of collaborations with 3rd parties, e.g. Joint Ventures, Joint Development Agreements, etc. You should aim to have some or a combination of these metrics in your overall business KPIs to monitor the effectiveness of your IP strategy implementation to judge whether the investment you are making in IP is adding value. Whichever metric(s) you choose, look to your business strategy for guidance.

CHAPTER 7

ON THE HOME STRAIGHT – THE ART OF LAUNCHING NEW PRODUCTS SUCCESSFULLY

So you have finally developed your new product. You have gone through all the project phases, you have followed the Phase Gate process to the letter, you have kept everyone involved and informed, you have regularly checked with customers that your new product is still relevant and that it meets all the targets set by the project definition document, large scale production capability is now in place, with all the necessary quality controls and standard operating procedures. Now for the final stage of this long process, you are now going to transform your new technology into profit. What could possibly go wrong?

If you have got your project this far, then you have likely spent a lot of company money to get here, you have involved a lot of different people from different job functions, and you have personally given a hell of a lot to it.

This project may have been a big part of your life for many months, and often for several years. At times it will have felt like you would never get to the end given so many barriers, so much hard work. But finally you are here and everyone involved, from the project team to the executive team is excited and looking forward to sales starting to roll in. Aren't they? You will still unfortunately find some doubting voices at this stage, particularly if you haven't been able to address all the barriers listed in Chapter 2. You may find some jealousy that your project has succeeded this far when others haven't, and that it is getting all the attention and pulling in the funding. You may find some apathy from senior management, individuals whose pet project wasn't the one chosen for resourcing, and may well be happy to see you crash and burn with your new product so they can say 'I told you it wouldn't work', even though it's their business as well that will be failing, their profits that will be affected. Strange, but that's the way some people behave, that's 'people & politics'. But push on, keep reading and you will overcome all this and deliver success.

Like many of the aspects of new product development and innovation discussed in this book, there are many great publications on how to successfully launch new products. Often these are written and researched from the retail and consumer market point of view, but many concepts are still relevant to the industrial markets that I am focusing on in this book. Again, my intent in this chapter is to offer my personal experience of 30 years of working in TTIP, and offer advice on what is important, what works and what doesn't, and the barriers you will likely encounter in launching new products into B2B markets.

Pre-Launch

The first thing you need when launching your new product is a commercial champion. Up to this point, your project is still likely to be considered the property of the technical or R&D department, as the project leader is likely to have been a technical lead, and project team meetings will have focused for much of the time on technical matters, as the period to develop, test and productionise the new technology and new product takes up the bulk of the project time. Whilst that view still remains in the business, everyone else in the organisation will continue to view the new product as some kind of unproven prototype, with an element of risk surrounding it. This is why handover of project ownership is critical. Up to this point, your commercial team members will likely have acted almost as consultants on the project team, offering advice and information to guide the project and keep development on track and relevant. Some of them will have done practical work in terms of taking you or your technical team to customers, for application discussions or product trials, but they will generally feel they are just the door openers in these situations, and that it is the technical person that will still be taking the lead.

Sales people are generally very nervous about launching new products and many will not want to touch it until it is 100% fool proof in their eyes. They do not want to be the guinea pig, they want someone else to debug it first. As we have explored in earlier chapters, sales people fall into two types, hunters and farmers. The hunters are the ones that thrive on developing new business opportunities, seeking out new customers and new applications. Farmers are the ones that prefer to visit the same customers and distributors again and again, building strong long term relationships as channel managers. Both types are needed in a business, both types are important, but obviously for launching a new product, you are much more likely to get a hunter interested and on your side, so it is important you understand the sales team and who best to influence and engage to support customer trials (Chapter 4) and to be your ambassadors for the new product launch.

A new product launch will always go much smoother if ownership of the newly developed product is picked up by someone in senior sales management, because this gives much more credibility to the sales team that the new product is 'okay' for launch and isn't still a prototype to debug. But this is easier said than done. When a technical lead has owned a project for sometimes many years, it is very difficult for the person to give away their baby to someone else. They have worked extremely hard on getting the project to where it is, and they naturally want to be rewarded for their hard work. There is a tendency to feel in this situation that you have to be the one that retains ownership, so that the sales and growth will still be associated with you and is something important and tangible you can bank when reviewing your performance with your boss. I know this because I have been there and I have had that attitude. But over time I learnt this was a mistake, because when you as the project technical lead retains ownership you find you are constantly struggling with your own sales team during the launch, rather than spending your energy on pitching to customers. I discovered it made things much easier and created much less internal politics if I handed the project over to a senior sales figure for commercialisation. The flip side of this is that the senior sales lead does not usually feel very comfortable about taking on something which they have the same reservations and concerns about as their own sales teams (see earlier), but that is what management is all about, at some point you just have to suck it up and take responsibility because that is the best thing for the company. The only way I found to achieve this reliably is to have built a strong personal relationship over the life of the project (or many projects) with the senior sales person, building trust. And you have to have numerous open and direct conversations with this person about the upcoming need for the transfer of project ownership, so everyone is aware that it is coming down the line. Once ownership is transferred, the previous project technical lead needs to be seen to take an active step backwards and move into a support role. Essentially, roles become reversed. Before getting to the launch the technical person was leading, with sales in a consultancy role. At the commercialisation phase, the sales lead should take the lead role, with technical acting as consultant. The senior commercial lead has to be seen to organise the pre-launch presentations and meetings, co-ordinate the launch itself and the program of customer roll out, otherwise the sales team will see through this as just a front and not change their point of view.

Another key element you need to consider as your project moves from the productionisation to the commercialisation phase is, at what point should you celebrate success? You and your project team have all worked very hard to get to the point of commercialisation. You have all achieved something amazing together, with significant progress in terms of technology and benefits for your customers, is this not worth celebrating? Celebrating success is a really useful way of helping everyone take a breather, to stand back and feel they have all done a great job together, because this can be a great motivator and re-energiser. We all like recognition and reward, and celebrating milestones in any team work is a great way to give everyone, including yourself, the recognition and reward they deserve for a job well done and is fantastic for team bonding. The celebration event can be in many forms, a BBQ lunch, a team dinner, an announcement in the company newsletter or in town hall addresses by senior management or the CEO, personal gifts from the company, one off bonus payments, or my personal favourite (be warned if you ever work for me), a karaoke evening (sorry, too many years living in China I'm afraid), though you'll have to do the latter on a Friday night as there will be too many sore heads the following morning! What style of celebration you choose will depend on the size, complexity and geographical spread of your project team.

But when to celebrate? The sales dollars aren't in the bank yet. Shouldn't we wait until sales reach a threshold level? But that might take 12 months or more, too long to keep people pumped about pushing this project over the top to completion. I prefer to celebrate around the product launch event. It can be part of the event, involving your invited customers, or usually a separate internal celebration. You can judge the form, nature and timing of the celebration, but please make sure you do something. It will go a long way to re-invigorating the team and creating the energy for the final push for commercialisation and sales growth.

Another behaviour you will observe once you get close to product lunch is 'Jumping on the Bandwagon'. Leading up to this, there will be plenty of doubters along the way as your project progresses, as it hits difficult challenges, or misses occasional milestones, and efforts have to be redoubled to get back on track. You will hear things like 'it doesn't work,' 'it will never work,' 'I told you it wouldn't work,' 'I never thought it was a good idea in the first place,' etc. You will hear lots of such negative language along the way, all designed to pull you down, de-energise and demotivate the team, and make your job harder. From inside the team, such comments are usually only expressed outside of project meetings, in the corners of coffee rooms, as these types of people rarely have the balls to speak out like this in meetings. From outside the team, these will be people on the side-lines of a project, who don't know the full story and are just formulating their opinion on misinformation and gossip. This is basically another version of the 'Idea Killer' (see Chapter 2) that we can call the 'Project Killer', but it is a much more subtle and subversive challenge, because the Idea Killer is very much spoken upfront, whereas the 'Project Killer' is only spoken in quiet corners in smaller groups. You have to deal with such subversive politics using your leadership skills. Keep positive, keep listening, keep the team involved, and keep communicating at all levels. Eventually, if you follow the guidelines for TTIP, your project will progress well, your new product will move into the commercialisation phase and the business will start to gear up for the product launch and sales campaign. At this stage, it is amazing how many of those same people who whispered in quiet corners suddenly start to join in the growing number of conversations within your business about how good the new product is and how excited people are about the launch. This is 'jumping on the bandwagon'. Plenty of people don't want to be involved in all the hard work of making something a success, but they sure want to be associated with the success once they see it coming. You should simply ride with this and see this as a positive thing, as it is a clear sign that your new product has developed a positive buzz within your organisation and that you are making excellent progress in selling your new product internally to your organisation. This then only serves to energise and fuel the push for external commercialisation out in the market place.

The Big Launch

So what about the product launch campaign itself? You need to pitch this right or all your hard work up to this point will be wasted. You need the right content, you need the right channels, you need the right spokesperson, and of course you need receptive customers to pay attention to your message.

During my 30 year career I have lived through the incredible rise of the digital age. When I first started work, no one had a laptop, office desktops were still considered luxury items for people at work, and many of my colleagues were still writing reports by hand, and giving them to a secretary to type; seems unbelievable now. But very quickly desktop computers became the norm, then over the years, everyone started getting a laptop, then a smartphone as well. Outside of the office, the digital revolution saw the rise of the internet and this has had a profound effect on how media is used to launch products now. Product launches used to be all about brochures and mailshots, followed by customer launch sessions. These days, brochures and printed media do still have a place but almost as an afterthought. Product launches also used to be more discrete events in the past, with launch dates, what is now called a 'Hard Launch'. But given the use of social media to send out teasers, soft launches are becoming more prevalent. These allow time to build up market interest and expectation, but need close management. Soft launches are projects in themselves and need strong leadership, a clear timeline and a dedicated team to make them happen and keep the momentum going. You can gauge best from your market and customer knowledge for your project, but for me, a combination of 'Soft Launch' with some targeted, regional launch events is generally my preference.

The number one thing that has not changed is the need for launch events, though these can be multimedia and to some extent done virtually if necessary. Launch events are vital so that you can get in front of your customers and interact on a face to face basis to pitch your new product. Social media such as LinkedIn or Twitter are used frequently nowadays as a route to tease the market about new product launch events. And when I talk about the market, I mean all points along the supply chain, not just customers. You need to speak to your distributors as well as the end users, otherwise you will have your customers asking about a new product that your distributor knows nothing about, a potentially embarrassing disaster for a new product launch. You need to train your sales team and lead speaker at the event all about the new product. Adverts still have a place in trade magazines, etc., but everyone is now so wrapped up with checking their social media accounts on an hourly basis these days that this route has become the predominant method of informing your markets about your new products, and specialist marketing digital media roles have grown up in businesses to manage this. Such roles usually manage your web site, as well as your web presence.

As far as getting the right content, this is all about focusing your launch media (through all its many forms) on features versus benefits. Sure, you should tell your audience what the product is, but what you're really selling is what it does. How is it going to add value to your customers? Your new product will typically do one or more of five things for an end user 1) improve their product or process safety, 2) improve their product performance, 3) improve their process cost effectiveness, 4) lower their direct process cost, and/or 5) meet new or upcoming market regulations. So you can normally group and orient your pitch towards focusing on one or more of these five aspects. I have never seen a new product benefit that could not be fitted into one or other of these 5 categories. It is important to remember that these things are really the only things that matter to the customer and it is revealing to note that they mainly play to benefiting a customer's process. In B2B markets, every product that a customer purchases is to help them perform one of their processes, be it the process of manufacturing their own goods, the process of handling sales orders, the process of servicing their customers, the process of keeping their employees safe in the work place, etc. Many will be physical processes, using physical products, but some processes will be virtual if your business is about developing software. It is important to remember that your customer is doing something with your product, in combination with lots of other products. Your product has to fit into their process or help them redefine a new process to replace the old one. The tougher it is for them to integrate into their own processes, the harder will be the sell.

As the 5 types of new product benefits are so fundamental to commercialising a new product successfully, let's explore them in more detail;

1) Improved product or process safety – your new product may offer a safer alternative to an existing product, e.g. a lighter weight for a worker to lift, or reduced VOC content, or more ergonomic design, or better anti-slip properties, etc., or it may do away completely with the need for the current product

used, by engineering out the need for using it. Or it may allow the customer to manufacture a safer product. Such safety benefits, in my experience have become the number one benefit that all businesses are looking for worldwide, due to a continuing rise in worker safety governance, operator safety regulations, and the general increased duty of care for employees. Safety is often the number one selling benefit to build into your product design during the project definition. You should be scouting for such opportunities in your chosen markets when seeking new product and service opportunities.

2) Improved product performance – your new product may allow your customer to manufacture a more superior product, e.g. a more fuel efficient car, or a faster processor chip, enhancing their selling proposition to their own customers. This kind of benefit is excellent for partnering with customers at the design phase early on in a project.

3) Improved process cost effectiveness – your new product may offer your customers the ability to enhance the indirect benefits of running their own processes, such as improving the yield of their manufacturing process. It may be that your solution actually costs them more than their current solution, or that they have to invest capital expenditure to implement your solution, but the improved yield more than offsets the cost increase, thus proving a saleable solution. So this benefit category targets the indirect cost of process improvement, enhancing process cost effectiveness. This is a little different and more subtle than Category 4, which targets direct cost reduction for the customer, though the two are usually inter-related.

4) Lower direct process cost — the most simple and straightforward benefit that a new product can offer to a customer is simply to be a lower cost shoe-in for an existing product. The customer doesn't have to change anything about what they do, just start buying your product and save money. This might be fine if you are in the business of copying products when their patent runs out, but this is absolutely not the approach to take if you are trying to develop a new product for a potential new opportunity that you have identified. But it happens, and it may be a consequence of your new product costing considerably less to manufacture than the product it replaces, but if you do this, then you have simply got your pricing wrong and you are giving away profit. More likely in this category is that your new product allows the customer to change their process in some way that lowers their direct cost, e.g. use less raw material, use less manpower, do something faster or cut out process steps all together, etc.

5) Meets new or upcoming market regulations — businesses are generally pretty switched on to regulations that impact them in terms of keeping their plants operating (e.g. environmental emission and waste disposal regulations) and in doing business in the markets they serve (e.g. National Food and Drug approvals). An ongoing trend in many markets is that such regulations tend to get stricter over time, e.g. allowable factory emission levels get lower over time. So businesses naturally have to keep up with such regulations in order to continue doing business, which means they need technological and engineering solutions to meet the imposed limits. As a new regulation comes down the line, this presents

opportunities for new products and new processes to be developed, and if you can offer something new to help them meet the new regulation, then that is a great selling proposition.

These 5 categories are not mutually exclusive, and your new product, even if it was developed primarily with one particular benefit in mind, will often display a combination of two or more of these benefit categories. This is where you need to understand your customer's and the market's needs well so that you can focus your benefit sell on to what is most important to them. It is interesting to note, that these 5 categories of benefits mirror the 5 Market trends that are used in the Technology Roadmapping process discussed in Chapter 3. This should be expected, because if you are developing a new product to service a targeted market trend, then the product you develop should display all the benefits required to meet that market trend.

It is important in your new product sales pitch to get the balance right between focusing on features versus benefits. Whilst certain members of your audience may find facts about the features of your new product interesting, don't labour too much on the science behind the features, as there will always be a section of the audience that will have very little interest in what it is and particularly not in the science behind it all. Just say enough to explain the background, and give credibility to what you are pitching, otherwise you run the risk of turning off a large portion of your audience. This can show as a business that you are the market experts and you know what you're talking about, but this is all just a forerunner towards the big pitch on the benefits of your new product.

To add further credibility to your new product launch media content and launch event, you should consider whether there are any independent 3rd party individuals or organisations that you can bring in. Are there any relevant approvals needed, regulatory bodies or other market influencers you could partner with to endorse your new product?

Post Launch

After the launch, you will need to continue to budget for the fact that some of your people will be spending their time providing technical support to the sales team for some time. Despite the pre-launch training for the sales team, they still need to gain confidence in talking about the product to customers, and having a technical expert at their shoulder when they are doing it will go a long way to building their confidence and give them a safety net for answering any particularly difficult questions from the customers. But the process of handover is important to keep in sight. At some point, the sales team must be able to handle the new product on their own out in the market place, such that it eventually becomes a standard product. It is another strange phenomenon I have observed in business that new products continue to be considered 'new' for many years internally, and the mind-set that it is still something new pervades for a long time, sometimes several years. All technically based products have some element of continuous improvement surrounding them, so all products whether existing or newly launched can have a feel to them that this is just the latest version on a long road of product and technology evolution. Even products that have been around for decades.

This is one of the challenges with new product development, when is the product actually developed? When is the process complete? Improvements can be made continuously, and there is always a contingent in the project team that wants to keep going and improve, improve, improve. That is where the project definition and the targets you set right at the start are so important. Keep referring to them and keep validating these with the target customer base and once you have achieved the targets you stop, very clear cut. At that point the new product is saleable and will make money for you. It is easy to get carried away with the science of the project and just keep making improvements because you've thought of yet another way of making it perform better. But you have to keep reminding people that this is a business, you are all there to make money, so keep everything in perspective. Further improvements to the new product you have just developed is another new project that needs to go into the ideas list for assessment against all the other new ideas. Maybe you will choose to work on it, maybe you won't. This has to be a business decision, not a project team decision. This type of product and technology evolution forms the basis of one type of Technology Roadmap (Chapter 3).

And finally, make sure you follow up and review your project sometime after the launch and the initial sales are coming in. Post-launch there is usually a feeling from the project team that their job is done and it's time to start work on the next project, after all, it's handed over to the sales team now, so surely it's their responsibility? Whilst it's true that the team are unlikely to all be spending the same amount of time they were on the project prior to the launch, there are many things that need to be followed up to ensure that the project is truly a success. Are revenue and growth meeting your expectations? Are production costs as expected? Is product performance matching expectations? Any quality complaints? Any production capacity, material supply or distribution issues? Many things can still work to bring your newly launched product down or at least suppress what might otherwise be a very successful product. Post-launch project team meetings are therefore vital to manage the product through its first few months (and sometimes longer) in the market. A formal Post Launch Review is also the final phase of the Phase Gate project management system (Chapter 4). If you have been the project leader for most or all of the long period of the project, you will want to see it through and guide it as much as you can to success. You will want the numbers to demonstrate to your boss and the Executive that this has been a success. This may be something that ends up on your CV, so it matters to your future, to the future of you project team and to the future of the business.

What Can Possibly Go Wrong?

It is well documented that most new product launches fail and I have seen this first hand too many times. Below is what I have learnt from the failures I have seen;

1) Believing too much in the hype of your own product – have you really done all the testing? Have you checked that it is safe? Does it really deliver everything that it needs to? Do you understand the limitations, what it cannot do versus what it can? Have you tested the boundaries of what will make it fail or perform out of specification (e.g. environmental use limits)? Have you done enough end user testing? Does it meet customer expectations? Are the original target parameters you designed against still valid in the market? Listen to your customers, not to your own internal voice and

not to the voice of your internal organisation. Did you genuinely have robust market data to justify developing the product in the first place? (see Chapter 2), if not, have you developed a 'white elephant'?

2) Launching before it is truly ready – this can lead to disappointment and bad press and is difficult to come back from if you've given your product a bad name. When a project has been going for a while and progress is good and you have developed the technology and prototyped the new product, then there is always mounting excitement in the business (which is great), but along with the excitement there is also a mounting pressure to push forward and launch, particularly after one or two successful scale up trials in production. Even though the technology and prototype may be sound, and hitting all the Phase gate targets, if the product is still not fully quality control compliant, don't launch, you will regret it once the first quality complaint comes in. Such a phase in a project requires handling cleverly. You want to maintain the enthusiasm from the business, but also manage the expectations, particularly at Board level.

3) Not enough resources put into a launch and sales support – you need to appreciate that the business will likely need to take a loss on the new product for a while as you work to establish the product in the market. This should form part of your project costs and should not be ignored as it can be a significant contribution to the total costs of developing a new product. Launch pricing is key here, and usually the subject of much debate within the commercial and business leadership. You don't want to give away all

your hard earned technology, but you also don't want to price it out of market expectation. It is always essential to focus on value rather than price, after all these are technically differentiated products that should be delivering something unique to your customers, so any new products should be able to pay for themselves quickly. So price should not be a big issue and should certainly not be high up in any conversation you have when pitching it to customers. Also, you need to make sure you have the manufacturing capacity to handle sales as volume ramps. Once you hit a certain threshold of sales, you will run out of manufacturing capacity. You need to be very clear about what this level is and judge when this is likely to occur, because you are going to need capex investment to build more capacity and this takes time to implement. You need to be working closely with Operations and Sales to manage production capacity and customer delivery expectations. In very successful product launches, you will need to manage customer expectations closely to avoid major delivery delays if you don't get capacity planning right.

4) The product may be ahead of its time – is your chosen market really ready for it? At one stage in my career, I worked as Global Technology Director for the largest supplier of Foundry Crucibles in the world. We produced the most sophisticated, high performance consumable products on the market, offering service lives measured in months. We monitored a growing foundry casting market in the Far East and every year at the Board we would discuss whether the time was right for us to enter the Chinese market. When we did our market research,

what we discovered was that although there was a growing foundry market in China, most of these foundries were small and unsophisticated, to the point that users would smash off the crucible to get the metal out, so to this market, the crucible was a cheap, single use, one shot consumable. But our product cost several orders of magnitude more than the cheap, single shot version they were using. There was no way such end users would gain any benefit from using our sophisticated products and a product launch in China at the time would have been commercial suicide for us. And so we recognised that if we wanted to enter this market, we first needed to educate the market in the use of our products, such that end users could learn that by proper handling and cleaning, they could extend their crucible life by many months, gaining significant process cost benefit and decreasing their US$/kg for cast metal considerably. This is basically the type 3 category (improved process cost effectiveness) new product benefit discussed earlier. Essentially, our technology was ahead of its time for the Chinese foundry market, and so we set about a market education program for 2 years before we finally built a factory there and entered the market proper.

5) The product may be too complicated to use – you cannot impose too many use limitations and rules surrounding the use of your new product, otherwise this will hinder take up by the end user. For rugged industrial products, a new product must be built with some level of mishandling in mind to cope with the nature of some of the rugged environments it may encounter. This is particularly relevant for market sectors where there is a lot of outside working such

as mining or oil & gas.
6) Product development was technology led and not market led – your product may be interesting, but does it really have a market? I have heard many debates about technology led versus market led products. Maybe your new product creates a new category of product, in which case it will need a big market education exercise before you can hope to convince the market of its benefit and value. If it's a new category of product, is the market segment really clear?
7) Not clearly communicating the benefits versus the features – people often get confused by this when preparing product launch presentations.
   a. Every time I have launched a new product I have also had to coach the person preparing the launch documents in the art of defining Features versus Benefits. This is partly a result of the internal barrier of technical jargon (see Chapter 2), because when the technical targets of a project get mixed up with the technical jargon in a company's culture and language, confusion arises, e.g. if a project has been focused on 'reducing the content of impurity X in our product from 4% to 2% ', and then this is achieved, everyone thinks, way hay, we have now got a product with only 2% impurity and they start plastering this all over the launch literature as a 'benefit'. In this case the technical challenge may have been considerable, so very well done to the team, but there is a big risk that all their good work can easily be sold short if every time I have to explain to the person preparing the product launch literature, that customers don't care about impurity X, they only

care about what the product does for them. In this case, reducing impurity X improved thermal insulation properties by 20%, delivering huge energy savings to the end user, that is the benefit. You have to be very clear about splitting the new aspects of a product into features versus benefits. If your team is confused, so will the customer be.

b. My guidance to people on 'features versus benefits' is very simple. When looking at a list of characteristics of the new product and deciding which ones are features and which ones are benefits, just consider my simple advice throughout this book in terms of prioritising TTIP 'Focus on what it does, not what it is'. What it does = Benefits, what it is = Features. Features will include all those type of characteristics that define what a product is, e.g. chemical composition, morphology, colour, form, etc. Trickier is when people are presented with a list of technical numbers about a new product, e.g. thermal conductivity, electrical conductivity, viscosity, density, dimensions, weight, etc. These are all the kind of things which typically end up on a product data sheet. Non-technically minded people tend to see some of these as benefits because these characteristics were the targets of the project to develop the new product, but these are all actually still features because they are simply another way of expressing 'what it is'. I have seen people struggle with this concept many times. If you are in the business of selling insulation, then they think having a thermal conductivity of half the previous product is a benefit, but in terms of how you need to market your product it is not, it is a feature, but it is absolutely the feature that delivers the benefit of improved insulation that saves energy costs and reduces CO2 emissions for your customers.

   c. In terms of how you need to market your new product to customers and end users, usually these people will not think in terms of data sheet numbers (e.g. thermal conductivity), they will think in terms of product use and their own internal company language, which in the example above, will be insulation and ultimately energy savings, because that is what insulation is there to do. In preparing your sales pitch you can absolutely say that because the new product has half the thermal conductivity of the old product (= the Feature) then it delivers improved insulating properties and saves energy costs and reduces CO2 emissions to the customer (= the Benefits). Do not confuse the two concepts, because customers will see through your logic and you can lose credibility. Certainly, all the long list of features of the new product are important to understand clearly, because it is this unique blend of features, that you have spent a lot of time and money developing, which deliver all the benefits.

8) Not keeping abreast of competitor activity – do you know what new technologies and products your competitors are working on? Pretty embarrassing if they are working on something similar and they launch before you.

9) Not having all the necessary regulatory approvals – this is particularly important if you are trying to move

into an adjacent market that is new to your business. Make sure you hire an expert or a consultant in the field.

Success and your Next Steps

So, you have made it. You have worked through the TTIP process, you have struggled against and overcome many challenges. Your new product has been embraced by the sales team, championed by sales management and customers love it. It delivers exactly what they needed (whether they knew it or not), end users cannot imagine doing their jobs now without your product. The production costs are within expectations, and the profits are starting to roll in. Well done, you should feel pretty smug about yourself. You have achieved something that few people have in business and you should feel proud. Hopefully, your success will lead to career progression, financial reward and a lot of personal satisfaction.

So where next? On to the next project? Would you take the same approach you did with TTIP next time? I doubt it. The process described in this book is the culmination of 30 years of trying things out, making mistakes, seeing things from different perspectives, bouncing ideas off people, listening to feedback and input. You will almost certainly be doing the same. The process described here is also an idealised process, it is what I would like to follow every time with a project, but reality hits you with challenges all the time, some you have seen before, some unexpected, all of which means no project ever goes smoothly through the processes I have guided you through. So ask yourself, what have you learnt from your successful project, how does it compare to the process described in this book, what challenges did you face that are listed here?

Did you find new ways to overcome them? Are there any new situations you encountered? What would you do differently next time? How would you improve the process of Transforming Technology into Profit?

Or maybe it's time for a career change? Perhaps you would like to see TTIP from the perspective of another business function? I chose to do exactly this in my career and it proved a very valuable exercise, it gave me great new perspectives that helped shape significantly the processes and concepts described in this book. It taught me that developing new products is not just a technology driven exercise and that commercial, financial and operational skills are just as important and necessary for success.

CONCLUSION

What have I learnt in my 30 years of 'Transforming Technology into Profit'? There is no one size fits all solution. Businesses are complex, markets are complex, people are complex, and it is not possible to have a single comprehensive, all-encompassing process that deals with all aspects of TTIP. Your process needs to be tailored to your business, to your culture, and to the markets and customers you serve. What I have certainly learnt about what works is that any processes you use and roll out around your organisation must be simple. For organisations that are multi-national, you have an extra layer of complexity. You have many languages, many different business practices and different cultural attitudes to deal with. Any process you roll out has to take all this into account, or it will fail or at best just become a box ticking exercise.

It is very important that all the tools and management systems used in a business complement each other. I have seen new management systems brought in that seem to exist in isolation from existing systems. I have frequently seen separate systems at play in businesses that don't (or can't) talk to each other, that don't share the same terminology, and that muddy where responsibilities lie. I have seen global systems overlay and duplicate what regional systems are trying to manage, adding administrative burden and leading to a box ticking culture. Someone at the very top needs to keep oversight of all these things, otherwise complexity and confusion will result. For TTIP, it should be absolutely clear to all what the process is, what the sequence of events is that an idea goes through, how it becomes a project and how that project progresses through to commercialisation. Everyone should be clear what tools are applied at each step and who has responsibility for each step. The diagram below draws together all the processes and project phases described in this book. Above all, what you need is leadership that has a deep understanding of the process of TTIP and ownership. One person must own the whole process from the top, such that they can guide the organisation through all the steps effectively.

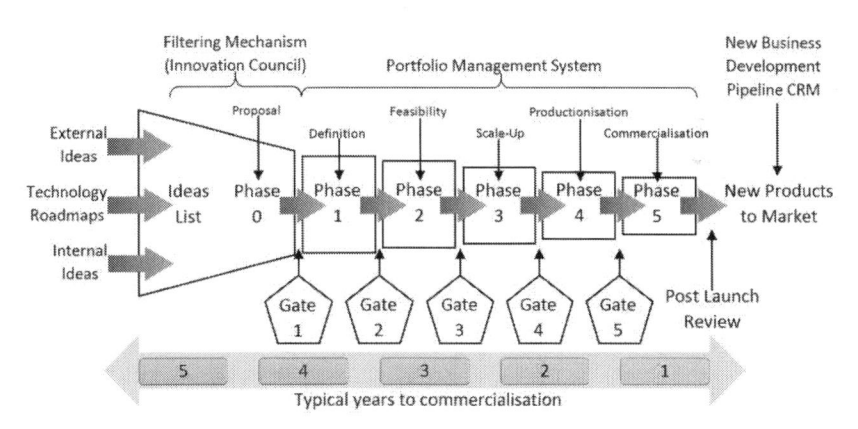

So what have you learnt about TTIP from reading this book? Yes, it is a complex process. There are many things you need to know, many skills you need to develop yourself and skills you will need to have in your team. You will have to overcome many challenges, you will need to influence many people, there will be plenty of frustration and plenty of battles along the way, but the rewards are tremendous. When you deliver a successful new technology project you and your team will feel elated, you will feel you have made a difference, and your success will lead to business growth, pay rises, career progression. All of these things make the hard work and frustrations well worth it.

I had said throughout this book that I love making one-page guides, summaries of complex things, so that I can see all the important aspects of a subject on one page and get my head around them. So to conclude this book, I offer you my summary of the key aspects of TTIP that you should keep in mind when you put this book down and go back to your work.

To lead new ideas through the complexities of the corporate world and transform them into successful new products, my 12 step advice checklist is that you need to;

1) Look to your business strategy for direction
2) Practice your leadership skills constantly
3) Finish your Project Definition completely before launching into any project
4) Remember to 'Keep it simple'
5) Be realistic about the resources you will need – don't overcommit
6) Get to know your team & the players in your business
7) Keep in contact with your customers frequently
8) Remember to 'Keep it relevant'
9) Communicate project progress frequently; up, down and sideways
10) Put your customer first in everything you do
11) Focus on 'what it does, not what it is'

12) Persevere, you will get there in the end

I mentioned in the Introduction to this book that Business is all about the 3Ps; 'People, Politics and Process,' and this book has been about how best to handle each of these aspects when you are involved in innovation, new product and new business development. But in an ideal world, business should all really be about the 3Cs; 'Customers, Customers, Customers'. If we can learn to put customers first in our own mind, in the mind of our teams and in the culture of the business within which we work, only then will the process of TTIP become a whole lot easier.

I hope you enjoyed the book and I hope you feel you have learnt something. All the opinions and observations I have expressed in this book are the summation of what I have learnt over a very long career, 30 years and counting, in the business of TTIP. You may not agree with them all, but I hope at least that they have given you a different point of view and offer food for thought. My intent is to spark debate and continue the dialogue on this important topic. Only then can we continue to improve and refine the process of TTIP.

Another thing I have also learnt in my 30 years, is that you never stop learning. This book is a summary of my current thinking, about how all the pieces of the puzzle I have picked up over the years have fallen into place. I certainly learnt a lot about TTIP in my first 25 years, but it was particularly in the last 5 years, when I was working at the corporate strategic level that all these parts started to fall into place. This is when I could start to get a much better overall picture of how the different parts of the process interfaced with each other and to appreciate how all the mistakes I'd made and the successes I'd enjoyed over the years started to fit into place. But I appreciate that this is only my current thinking, my current view. As I continue to put into practice the techniques I have outlined in this book, and I interact with new colleagues and new customers, and have the opportunity to discuss the processes I have mapped out in this book with fresh minds, my perspective will evolve, will change and I'm sure that in another 5 years' time I will have learnt more about TTIP and have more to say. To this end, I encourage you to send me your comments on what you have read here, so that together we can refine and improve this process further and help businesses all round the world to better develop more profitable, better performing products that make a real difference to the world and the quality of all our lives.

Finally, I wish you well on your career journey. I hope you get as much fulfilment, enjoyment and reward from your career in TTIP as I have.

Good Luck,

Andy

ACKNOWLEDGEMENTS

None of this would have been possible without all the great people I have worked with over the years. Great friends and colleagues that have influenced me, that I have learnt a lot from about Transforming Technology into Profit, about business and about myself, and that have been great sounding boards to bounce my thoughts and ideas off on the concepts in this book. People like Gary Latter, Craig Freeman, Robin Mottram, Ian Robb, Steve Chernack, Gary Jubb, Jason Street, Ben Tang, Jim Hick, Mike Murray, and Reynaldo 'Tito' Pereira (aka Mr Spreadsheet). These are people who are not only good at what they do, but they also care about what they do and understand the value of friendship and team work. Long may they prosper.

I'd also like to pay tribute to several people who have guided and mentored me during my career, I'd like to thank Martin Moore, who took me under his wing early in my career and taught me the ways of international business, and Phil Wright, who gave me my first big break that set me on a great career path.

I would also like to thank Stefan Kukula, Chief Executive of The Engineering Equipment and Materials

Users Association, for his useful comments, critique and valuable feedback as my reviewer of the first draft of the manuscript for this book.

ABOUT THE AUTHOR

Dr Andy Wynn has spent over 30 years in industry, working all over the world in industrial engineering and advanced materials manufacturing businesses. He gained BSc (hons) and PhD degrees in Chemistry, both at the University of Warwick (UK), the latter sponsored by the UK Atomic Energy Authority.

His career long passion has been 'Transforming Technology into Profit', creating new technologies and building new businesses from them. He has led many business functions during his career, including technology, general management, operations, sales and business development, including over 6 years based in China, and 5 years of C-level strategic leadership. He has published more than 40 technical papers and articles, and presented at numerous conferences around the world.

He has worked in a wide variety of industrial markets, including petrochemical, energy and renewables, metals, automotive, aerospace, rail, semiconductor and medical devices. His career splits roughly into 3 parts;

1) The first few years he spent learning to work closely with customers all over the world, as an engineer and

technologist, to interpret their needs and develop new products and solutions to solve their problems and add value to their businesses.
2) The bulk of his career was spent gaining the skills required to run a business successfully, through a variety of business leadership roles – general management, operational and quality management, sales management, product management and marketing. This culminated in moving to China to build and launch a business from scratch.
3) More recently, his career advanced to the strategic level, sitting on the Board of several businesses in Asia and Globally as Chief Technology Officer of the largest Division of a billion dollar multi-national manufacturer of advanced material and industrial engineered solutions.

Following the publication of his new book 'Transforming Technology into Profit', Andy has launched a new consultancy business, TTIP Consulting Ltd, to help industrial businesses grow by accelerating their delivery of better, more profitable new products. More information can be found at www.ttipconsulting.co.uk.

In his spare time, Andy is very active and spends much of his free time in the gym or outdoors. He spent 17 years studying Kung Fu and has a black belt and is a licensed instructor. As middle age and injuries began to take their toll, he swapped Kung Fu for tennis and has been playing regularly for several years now.

Andy is an accomplished musician and singer and has been playing electric guitar since he was 16. His album 'Never Too Late' was released on Office Records in 2012, and is available on iTunes and many other digital media outlets.

Printed in Poland
by Amazon Fulfillment
Poland Sp. z o.o., Wrocław